The Pepper Pantry:

The Essential
Hot Spice Guide

Dave DeWitt, the Pope of Peppers

Terra Nova Books

SANTA FE, NEW MEXICO

Terra Nova Books

Published by Terra Nova Books, Santa Fe, New Mexico.
www.TerraNovaBooks.com

ISBN 978-1-484842-75-1

Contents

Introduction: Why Cooks Spice Up Their Food

There are many diverse theories about why cooks have added the spices in this book to their foods ever since the dawn of cooking:

- Spices make foods taste better;
- The "eat-to-sweat hypothesis": eating spicy foods makes us cooler during hot weather;
- To disguise the taste of spoiled food;
- Spices add nutritional value to food;
- The antimicrobial hypothesis: Spices kill harmful bacteria in food and aid in its preservation.

Which of these theories are correct?

Well, certainly not the "eat-to-sweat" hypothesis. If it's hot outside, you don't need a spice to induce perspiration—you'll already be sweating. And despite popular belief, spices were never used to cover up spoiled or rotting foods because cooks know they won't work for that use—the smell of the food turning bad would overwhelm that of the spices. The theories remaining—namely, making foods taste better, adding nutritional value (especially from chile peppers), and the antimicrobial hypothesis—are the correct answers.

But perhaps the most fundamental reason for the boom in spicy foods is a major shift in the way many Americans are eating. I spoke with food historian and author Liz Rozin about this subject. "When we look at the broad spectrum of human flavoring practices," she said, "we see one curious correlation. The heavier the dependence on plant or vegetable foods, the more pronounced the seasonings; the heavier the consumption of animal foods, the less pronounced the seasonings. Those cuisines that clearly demonstrate a highly spiced or complex seasoning profile—Southeast Asia, India, Africa, Mexico—all have long relied on high-plant, low-meat diets"

Of course, the U.S. was just the opposite: a culture that in its early days relied on beef, pork, and chicken as well as dairy foods. Vegetable foods in the U.S. were eaten primarily in the same regions where the cuisine was also the spiciest: the South and the Southwest. And at least three other major food trends have paralleled the move to spicy foods over the past two decades: natural foods, vegetarian foods, and low-fat foods. And meat consumption has declined as well, setting the scene for the modern return of Rozin's theory of why ancient, "less satisfying" foods were highly spiced: We need the heat and flavor of chiles and other spices to make up for the lack of the flavors of meat and fat in more-spartan cuisines. The new corollary of eating in the twenty-first century might be: "The healthier you eat, the more you need to spice up the food."

In this book, I focus on the most important spicy ingredients you need in your pantry to keep up with all these food trends!

PART 1

Roots: Ginger, Horseradish, and Wasabi

Ginger

BACKGROUND AND NOMENCLATURE

My first experience with ginger came in childhood: tasting my mother's homemade ginger snaps, those spicy cookies with just a hint of a bite. It was quite a few years later before I experimented with the freshly peeled root, but now, all forms of ginger find their way into my kitchen. I should point out immediately, though, that technically, ginger is not a root but rather a rhizome, an underground stem that looks like a tuber—or a thick root. And it is one of the most fragile of all the spicy ingredients because its heat fades so quickly, especially after processing and when cooked.

The etymology of the word ginger is originally from the Sanskrit *shringavera*, meaning "of horned appearance," an allusion to the shape of the rhizomes. It was transliterated to the Greek *ziggiberis* and then became *zingiber* in Latin, *ginibre* in early French, and *giniber* in Old English, from which we got "ginger."

It is a very early spice, maybe the oldest of all, dating to about 4000 B.C. A clue to its extreme age is the fact that it is grown only from a division of the rhizomes, and not from seed—an indication that it has been under human control for so long that it's lost the ability to propagate from seed—one of the few spices with this trait. Also, there is no evidence that cultivated ginger appears anywhere in a wild form.

THE PLANT AND ITS PUNGENCY

Ginger is part of the genus *Zingiber* of the family Zingiberaceae. The genus has about a hundred species of perennial plants, many of which are grown as ornamentals. The different species of *Zingiber* have many culinary uses: For example, the shoots and flowers of *Zingiber mioga*, the Japanese ginger, are used fresh or pickled as a flavoring in Japanese cuisine.

The principal cultivated ginger is *Zingiber officinale*, native to tropical Asia, which is a deciduous perennial with thick, branching rhizomes, upright stems, and long, pointed leaves. The flowers are quite lovely— yellow-green with purple and yellow lips. The plant can grow up to four feet tall.

There are many cultivated varieties, or cultivars, of spice ginger, and the rhizomes vary in color and pungency. In India, the favorites are "Cochin" and "Wynad Manantody," while in Jamaica, there are yellow ginger, or "Tambric," and three cultivars of blue ginger: "Frog," "Bulbous," and "Chinese Blue." In China, a favorite cultivar is "Canton." The flavor and heat level vary greatly, as Australian spice expert Ian Hemphill notes: "The flavour will be similarly tangy, sweet, spicy, and warm to hot, depending upon when it has been harvested, as to a large degree, early harvested ginger is sweet and tender, while later harvested rhizomes are more fibrous and pungent."

The volatile oils causing the pungency are gingerols and shogaols. The shogaols appear when ginger is dried, and they are much more pungent, so dried ginger is hotter than fresh. It also has less water, so the pungency is more concentrated. Gingerol is commonly used to treat poor digestion, heartburn, and motion sickness.

Two related plants that are used principally in Asian cuisines (especially Thai) are the galangals: greater and lesser. Both are members of the Zingiberaceae family but not the genus *Zingiber*. Greater galangal (*Alpinia galanga*) is spicy but not quite as pungent as ginger, and is usually ground with chiles and herbs to make the base seasoning mix of red and green curries. Lesser galangal (*Kaempferia galanga*) is hotter than greater galangal and is used as a spice in Indonesian cooking. If a recipe calls for either galangal, fresh ginger can be substituted equally for lesser galangal, but use twice as much ginger as greater galangal.

Grown commercially in tropical regions, ginger is a worldwide crop. The leading grower is India, followed by China, Indonesia, Nigeria, Nepal, Bangladesh, and Thailand. By contrast, Jamaica, a country famous for its ginger, produces about 620 metric tons only one-tenth the amount of the United States (where it is grown in Florida and Hawaii).

Ginger requires rich, well-drained, but not sandy, soil, neutral to slightly alkaline, in partial shade or full sun, and also needs high humidity. The plants must have a ten-month growing season to produce the largest number of rhizomes. The planted rhizomes should have an "eye," or growing node, like a potato. In home gardening, they can be planted in pots at least a foot in diameter or, in tropical climates, in rows two feet apart with the rhizomes a foot apart in the rows. In the north, they can be grown in full sun but in warmer regions in light shade. They are best planted in the warm regions of the Northern Hemisphere between February and May, and take about nine months to mature with large rhizomes. By then, the above-ground foliage will have turned brown and died back. With luck, there will be striking flowers, but these are uncommon with *Zingiber officinale.* Use of a 14-28-14 fertilizer is recommended for neutral soils, 18-18-18 for acid soils.

The rhizomes are taken periodically during the growing season for drying and for fresh usage because they have the least amount of fiber. The fresh, young rhizomes will keep in a cool, dry place for about three months, which means they can be shipped long distances. In many regions, such as Jamaica, production has fallen off because of the tedious hand labor needed to peel the rhizomes.

Preserving the Rhizomes

Basically, there are two methods of processing ginger. One is to preserve it in brine or syrup or in crystalized form. The other is to dry it and then, optionally, grind it into powder. The first step in preserving it is to brine the peeled young rhizomes in barrels in a series of salt solutions for about a week. To preserve ginger in syrup, the brined rhizomes are washed and soaked in cold water to remove the salt and then boiled—first in water and then in a sugar syrup several times until the rhizomes have absorbed a large amount of sugar. During the final boiling, the water boils off, leaving a very thick syrup. The rhizomes can be left in the syrup and bottled, or removed, drained, dried, and sprinkled with sugar to make the crystalized form.

Pickled ginger is made from fresh rhizomes that are sliced as thin as paper, then placed in a vinegar solution. The acetic acid in the vinegar turns the ginger pink. In Japan, pickled ginger is known as *gari,* and it is considered a palate refresher between courses, commonly served with sushi and sashimi.

Dried ginger is made from the more-mature rhizomes, which are peeled by the farmers and left to dry in the sun—not the cleanest method. Increasingly, ginger is being furnace-dried. After that, the rhizomes are ground into powder and bottled, then used to flavor cookies such as ginger snaps, cakes, chutneys, and sauces. There are two grades: cracked, which is usually used in pickling and canning recipes, and powdered. The finest-quality powdered ginger is a light buff color, and is free from fiber. To substitute fresh ginger for ground, use one tablespoon ground fresh ginger for 1/8 tablespoon dried, ground ginger. Do not substitute dry ginger for fresh in Asian dishes.

Ginger oil is processed from fresh ginger with pressure techniques, and is used in medicine, perfumery, and the production of cordials and ginger wine. The oil, which is pale yellow, amber, or light green, is used both externally to treat bruises and aches, and internally for nausea and motion sickness. A combination of oil and dried, ground ginger is used as a commercial food flavoring, spicing up candies and soft drinks such as ginger beer and ginger ale.

Ginger is a good source of vitamin A and calcium, and also provides iron, phosphorous, riboflavin, and some protein. One-fourth cup of sliced fresh ginger has 17 calories, 0.4 grams of protein, 3.6 grams of carbohydrates, 0.2 grams of fat, and 0.5 grams of fiber.

STORAGE

Fresh ginger can be stored unwrapped in the produce drawer of the refrigerator, but it lasts longer in zip bags. One interesting way to preserve the fresh rhizomes is to peel them, place them in a glass jar, and cover them with a dry sherry, which will keep them fresh for three or four weeks. Peeled rhizomes can also be frozen whole and stored in a zip bag. When you need to use a piece, cut it off still frozen to avoid repetitive defrosting. Commercial grated ginger should be stored in the refrigerator after opening. Ginger in syrup or crystalized will keep in the cupboard for more than a year. Dried ginger slices can be kept indefinitely in glass jars in the cupboard if they are not exposed to excessive humidity. Ground ginger can be kept tightly sealed in glass jars in a spice cabinet.

CULINARY USES

Fresh ginger is commonly used in spice and curry pastes, and has a tendency to neutralize fishy smells and flavors. It is also used in chutneys and pickles. A topping of freshly grated ginger perks up cooked vegetables such as carrots, yams, and greens. For mild heat, use 2 teaspoons per pound of vegetables, 1 tablespoon for medium, and 3 tablespoons for hot.

Ground ginger is commonly used in the baking of breads, scones, and cookies but also is found in puddings and baked vegetables and apples.

Ginger Recipes

SIMPLE CRYSTALIZED GINGER

It is not necessary to buy imported crystalized ginger, especially if you don't mind a little work in the kitchen. Here is a home preservation technique that produces a delicious treat. Make sure the ginger rhizomes are young and tender, not fibrous. Note: This recipe requires advance preparation.

> 1½ cups peeled and sliced ginger
> 1½ cups sugar

Combine the ginger and sugar along with 1/2 cup water in a saucepan, and bring to a simmer over medium heat. Gently simmer the mixture uncovered until the ginger is tender, about half an hour. Remove the ginger slices, and place them on a sheet pan.

Return the saucepan to the heat, and bring to a boil. Boil the syrup uncovered for fifteen minutes, until it is very thick.

Pour the syrup over the ginger slices and let them dry, turning daily until the sugar crystallizes. Depending on the humidity, this may take several days.

Yield: About 3/4 cup **Heat scale:** Mild

GINGER BEER

There are numerous recipes for making ginger beer. Some contain alcohol, and others don't. We've included one that will produce alcohol but doesn't take as long to ferment as if you were making "regular" beer. The goal here is to have lots of carbon dioxide, or CO_2, produced in a short period time. Once you see a steady fermentation in the liquid, the beer is bottled, stored, and ready to drink in a few days. Just as in making wine or beer, the yeast is multiplying rapidly while consuming sugar and giving off alcohol and CO_2 as byproducts. No matter how much filtering you do, there will be some sediment at the bottom of your bottles from the yeast and the ginger. You can drink it or just carefully pour the beer into glasses without disturbing the sediment. For additional questions about making beer, there are many books or websites you can consult—or your local beer-making supplier. Note: This recipe requires advance preparation.

  1 lemon
  1 pound sugar
  1½ ounces grated ginger
  1 ounce cream of tartar
  1 ounce brewer's or wine or champagne yeast
    (available at beer-making supply stores)

Finely peel the zest off the lemon, removing only the outer waxy layer. Reserve the peeled lemon.

Place the sugar, ginger, lemon rind, and cream of tartar into a bucket or large bowl. Heat 2 quarts of water to boiling in a large sauce pot over high heat. Pour the boiling water over the sugar mixture, add the juice from the reserved lemon, and stir well. Let the mixture cool to 70 degrees, and taste. This will be approximately the taste of the finished product. Now's the time to adjust the taste and add more ginger if needed. Remove a cup of the liquid, and stir in the yeast, then add the yeast mixture back into the liquid.

Cover the container with a clean cloth, being sure it can't touch the top of the liquid. Tie a string around the top of the container to secure the cloth, and leave it all in a warm place, around 70 degrees, for twenty-four hours to ferment.

Strain the liquid through a fine cloth, or skim off the froth from the top, and carefully pour out the liquid so as not to disturb the sediment at the bottom.

Pour the beer into sterilized bottles, cap, and store them in a cool dark place. The beer should be ready to drink after two to three days.

Yield: 2 quarts   **Heat scale:** Mild

MANDARIN ORANGE CHICKEN SALAD WITH SESAME GINGER DRESSING IN A CRISPY NOODLE BOWL

This entree salad not only combines a number of flavors but different textures as well. It's sweet, hot, slightly sour, a little bland, crisp, and crunchy—all in one dish. Shrimp or even grilled halibut or salmon can be substituted for the chicken or, if desired, omitted for a tasty vegetarian alternative.

2 boneless, skinless chicken breasts,
    grilled and cut in strips
1 pound Chinese wheat noodles
3 cups chopped cabbage
1 cup mixed baby greens
1 bunch chopped fresh cilantro
1 small can Mandarin orange segments, drained
1/4 cup sliced radishes
1/4 cup toasted, sliced almonds
Sesame oil
Vegetable oil for frying, peanut preferred

SESAME GINGER DRESSING:

3 tablespoons vegetable oil, peanut preferred
2 to 3 teaspoons sesame oil
3 tablespoons rice vinegar
3 Thai chiles, stems removed, minced
1 tablespoon grated ginger
2 teaspoons orange zest
1 teaspoon sugar
1 teaspoon soy sauce
1/4 teaspoon dry mustard
Yield: 1/4 to 1/3 cup

Combine all the dressing ingredients in a bowl, and whisk. Let the dressing sit for twenty to thirty minutes to blend the flavors.

To make the noodle bowl, heat about 4 quarts of water in a stockpot to boiling. Add the noodles, and boil for four to five minutes or until the noodles are done. Remove, drain, and rinse with cold water. Drain thoroughly, and sprinkle with a little of the sesame oil, then toss to coat. Divide the noodles into four equal parts, and stir the noodles to loosen and separate.

Heat a wok until hot, add the vegetable oil to a depth of 3 inches and heat to 360 degrees. Add one of the noodle bunches and, using a round, heat-proof bowl or can, push down on the noodles so they press up along the sides of the wok to form a bowl. Fry until the noodles are browned and the bowl holds its shape. Remove and drain on paper towels. Repeat with the remaining noodles.

Combine the cabbage, baby greens, and cilantro in a large bowl, and toss with the dressing to coat.

To assemble the salads, place a noodle bowl on each of four individual plates. Divide the cabbage mixture among the bowls. Garnish the plate with some of the orange segments. Arrange the chicken strips on top of the cabbage, and garnish with the radishes, remaining oranges, and almonds. Serve with additional dressing on the side.

Yield: 4 servings   **Heat scale:** Mild

SPICY GINGER GARLIC GREEN BEANS

This recipe is best prepared with Asian green or long beans, but any thin, fresh green bean will do. It's a sweet, hot, and crunchy dish with lots of flavor that almost begs to be served with plain white rice. Although the vegetarian black vinegar is not essential, it does add another layer of complex flavors that you don't get with another vinegar. These beans can be steamed ahead of time and kept cool. Prepare the rest of the meal, and then finish off the stir-fry before serving, or prepare the beans and cool, let stand at room temperature, and serve. They are good served either hot from the wok or at room temperature.

1 pound thin green beans or Asian long beans,
   cut diagonally into 2- to 3-inch pieces
1 tablespoon vegetable oil, peanut preferred
1 tablespoon grated garlic
1 tablespoon chopped ginger
Garnish of toasted sesame seeds

SAUCE:
2 tablespoon vegetarian black vinegar, or
   substitute rice vinegar (available in Asian markets)
2 teaspoons sugar
1/2 teaspoon crushed red chile such as piquin
1/2 teaspoon black sesame oil (available in
   Asian markets)
1/4 teaspoon ground white pepper

Combine all the sauce ingredients in a small bowl, stir to mix, and set aside. Put the green beans in a steamer, wok, or heavy saucepan along with 1/2 cup water; cover, and heat over high heat. Steam the beans until bright green and almost done but still crunchy. Remove, and drain off the water. If finishing off later, run the beans under cold water to stop the cooking process.

Heat the wok over high heat, and when hot, add the vegetable oil and heat more. Add the garlic and ginger, and stir-fry for a minute or two until fragrant. Return the green beans to the pan, and stir-fry until almost done.

Add the sauce ingredients to the pan, and continue to stir-fry until the sauce has thickened and coats the beans.

Place the beans in a serving bowl or platter, garnish with sesame seeds, and serve.

Yield: 4 servings   **Heat scale:** Hot

GINGER SCONES

Scones are a Scottish quick bread whose popularity has spread across the ocean to the U.S. They are similar to biscuits but richer, with a slightly cake-like texture. The name "scone" comes from the Stone of Destiny, where the ancient kings of Scotland were crowned. Scones usually contain moist additions such as currants, which are traditional, or ingredients such as ham, cheese, sun-dried tomatoes, and—often in the Southwest—green chile. These scones combine two forms of ginger, ground and crystallized, and are much moister than the traditional ones.

> 1 cup plus 2 tablespoons milk
> 2 tablespoons honey
> 4 cups unbleached flour
> 1/4 cup sugar
> 2 tablespoons baking powder
> 1 teaspoon salt
> 1 teaspoon ground ginger
> 1/2 stick butter, softened and cut into small pieces
> 1/2 cup crystallized ginger, finely chopped and
>   dredged in flour
> 1/2 cup raisins, dredged in flour

Preheat the oven to 400 degrees. Lightly oil a sheet pan.

Combine 2 tablespoons of the milk and the honey in a small saucepan over medium-low heat, and stir until the honey is dissolved. Remove from the heat, and keep warm.

Sift all the dry ingredients into a large bowl. Add the butter, and cut it into the dry ingredients, using either a pasty blender or two forks, until coarse crumbs are formed.

Add the crystallized ginger, the remaining milk, and the warm honey mixture to the flour, and gently mix just until a soft dough is formed. Do not overmix. Turn the dough on a lightly floured surface, and gently knead five times.

Roll out the dough to form a thick 8-inch square. Cut the square into quarters, diagonally. Cut each quarter in half to make triangles.

Place the scones one inch apart on the sheet pan.

Bake for fifteen minutes, or until they are lightly browned. Place them on a rack to cool, and serve warm or at room temperature.

Yield: 8 scones   **Heat scale:** Mild

GINGER ALE

There is a long version and a short version for making ginger ale. Since the long one involves boiling, straining, cooling, bottling, and resting, with the possibility of exploding bottles, we are going to go with the easy one. The ginger syrup can be prepared ahead of time and refrigerated for a day before use. Note: This recipe requires advance preparation.

    1/4 cup coarsely grated ginger
    1 cup sugar
    1 quart seltzer or sparkling mineral water
    1 to 2 tablespoons lime juice, fresh preferred
    Garnish of fresh mint sprigs

In a saucepan, add the ginger along with 2 cups water, and bring to a boil over moderate heat. Gently boil for five minutes, remove from the heat, cover and steep at room temperature for at least twelve hours.

Strain the mixture into a bowl through a sieve lined with a double layer of damp cheesecloth. Gather the cheesecloth together and squeeze it to extract as much of the liquid as possible from the ginger, then discard the solids.

Return the ginger liquid to the saucepan, add sugar, stir to dissolve, and bring to a boil over medium heat. Boil until reduced to 1 cup, about five minutes. Remove and cool. You can store the syrup in the refrigerator tightly covered for a few days.

To serve, pour the seltzer into a large pitcher and add the ginger syrup. Add lime juice to taste. Fill tall glasses with ice, pour the ginger ale over the ice, garnish with the mint, and serve.

Yield: 1 quart   **Heat scale:** Mild to medium

Horseradish

BACKGROUND AND NOMENCLATURE

My mother Barbara was an expert at roasting meats, and she prided herself on not overcooking them as so many of her neighbors did in the 1950s. Her pork was cooked medium, her leg of lamb medium-rare, and her standing prime rib of beef (a Christmas Day tradition) was rare and served with a powerful horseradish sauce. She had no idea she was carrying on a tradition that had originated many hundreds of years before—she just knew that her family loved the pungency of the horseradish served on the slices of rare beef.

The English word horseradish is thought to originate from "hoarse radish," meaning a radish that is "hoarse," or coarse and strong. The French term for it, *raifort*, means "strong root," certainly an apt description.

THE PLANT AND ITS POWER

Native to southeastern Europe, horseradish, or *Armoracia rusticana*, belongs to the crucifer family, which also includes radishes and mustard. Botanists believe that it originally grew wild in Russia, Poland, and Finland. It is an upright, stout perennial with a thick taproot and oblong, toothed leaves.

There are two types of horseradish, common and Bohemian. The common types have broad, crinkled leaves, and are considered superior, while the Bohemians have narrow, smooth leaves and better disease resistance. There are many cultivars, such as "Maliner Kren" and "Improved Bohemian" in the U.S. and "Bagamerer Delikat," "Danvit," "Pozna," and "Erlagen" in Hungary.

Horseradish is grown on about 3,000 acres in Illinois, Wisconsin, New Jersey, California, and Virginia in the U.S., as well as in many European countries.

Both commercial and home cultivation are easy, requiring only well-drained, rich soil with a lot of organic material. Treat the soil with aged manure, and that should be all the fertilizer you need. Horseradish can be grown in sun or partial shade, but select a garden site apart from your other vegetables because horseradish is invasive and will take over. It is difficult to eradicate once established because portions of the roots left in the ground will sprout and grow into new plants, which is the way to grow them—from root divisions. It can also be grown from seed, but the plant produces so few of them that it's easier to use a root clone.

Dig a hole a foot wide and as deep as the shovel. Plant the roots at a 45-degree angle in the hole so they can fully develop. The top of the root, where the plant will sprout, should be just protruding from the soil. Water the plant well afterward, and irrigate if needed during the hot months of summer.

Commercially, root pieces with a diameter of about three-quarters of an inch and a length of about 8 to 12 inches are planted in rows 30 to 36 inches apart and spaced about 20 inches apart in the rows. About 9,000 root cuttings per acre are required.

Once frost has killed the tops, harvesting can begin. C o m - mercially, horseradish roots are harvested with modified potato diggers which load them onto conveyor belts where most of the dirt is knocked off. Trucks carry the harvested roots to cold storage before processing. Yields are 7,000 to 8,000 pounds per acre, and in storage, the roots will keep for ten to twelve months if they are maintained at 30 to 32 degrees in a relative humidity of 90 to 95 percent.

In the home garden, the young leaves can be picked and used fresh or cooked like greens. The roots are harvested in the fall— they need frost for peak pungency, flavor, and color. The leaves are cut off about a week before digging up the roots by plowing or using a gardening fork. The roots are washed, and the lateral roots are removed, leaving the taproot for future planting.

Before processing, the picked roots are packed away from sunlight, which will turn them green. If you live in a warm climate, remove all the roots from the ground, treating the plant as an annual. Store the main taproot to be replanted next year in a zip bag in the refrigerator. The outer section of the root is the only part used, as the inner core is less pungent and is rubbery and difficult to grate.

When the root is cut, peeled, or scraped, cells are broken, and two components, sinigrin and myrosin, combine to form the volatile oil allyl isothiocyanate (AITC), which is identical to the oil from black mustard seeds. The result is an intensely pungent aroma and flavor that goes to the back of the throat and attacks the nasal membranes. In fact, AITC is so pungent that it can kill the bacteria *Listeria* and *Escherichia coli*. But AITC is not heat resistant, so it loses its pungency rapidly when placed in hot foods, and is not stable in cold water either. However, adding vinegar or other acidic ingredients like lemon juice greatly retards the hydrolysis of AITC and keeps the horseradish pungent. This is how grated ginger is processed for bottling.

A very pungent root that controls bacterial infections and lowers fever, horseradish has a lot of flavor and no fat. One tablespoon of prepared horseradish contains six calories, 1.4 grams of carbohydrates, 14 milligrams of sodium, 44 milligrams of potassium, 9 milligrams of calcium, and 5 milligrams of phosphorous.

FORMS OF HORSERADISH

When buying fresh roots, choose the ones without blemishes and that not sprouting. Generally speaking, the whiter the root, the fresher it is. Peel only what you are going to use, and grate or shred it in a food processor. Make sure your kitchen is well-ventilated, as the pungent oils are volatile. Dehydrated granules, flakes, or powder are readily available; just add vinegar to power them up.

Varieties of prepared horseradish include regular (grated horseradish with vinegar), cream style, and beet horseradish. Other products containing horseradish include mustards, cocktail sauces, other sauces, dips, spreads, relishes, and dressings.

STORAGE

The smaller roots can be stored in zip bags in the refrigerator for up to two weeks, or frozen for a couple of months. Grated or otherwise-processed horseradish should be kept in the refrigerator. The dried forms should be stored in sealed glass containers in the spice cabinet.

CULINARY USES

Horseradish preparations are usually served cold because so much pungency and flavor is lost when they are cooked. Often, horseradish is made into a sauce or paste and served with roast beef or cold meats like ham or corned beef. It is commonly served with fish in Europe; for example, in Norway, the grated root is mixed with whipped sweet and sour creams, vinegar, and sugar to make a sauce called *pepperotsaus* which is served with cold, boiled fish such as salmon. The French mix it into cream sauces with lemon juice. Vinegar is commonly combined with it. It also is mixed with green food coloring or powdered spinach and served as "wasabi." In Austria, freshly grated horseradish is mixed with grated sour apples and lemon juice to make a relish for fried or roasted meat.

Other uses of horseradish include:

- Adding it, plus hot sauce, to tomato juice for a morning bracer;
- Or to bloody marys, if you're so inclined;

- Mixing it with mustard to increase its strength;
- Adding it to scrambled eggs, omelettes, and hash brown potatoes;
- Grating a small amount into potato salad, coleslaw, or dips;
- Adding it to soups just before serving;
- Mixing it with prepared barbecue sauces;
- Mixing it with sour cream to add to mashed or baked potatoes;
- Adding beet juice to grated horseradish to brighten the color;
- Adding it to tartar sauce, seafood cocktail sauces, hollandaise sauce, mayonnaise, and salad dressings;
- Making a horseradish butter with mustard and a little yogurt.

Wasabi

When you go to your favorite sushi restaurant and are served the green paste called "wasabi," 99 percent of the time, you are being served imitation wasabi made from horseradish, Chinese mustard, cornstarch, and blue and yellow food coloring. This is because real wasabi is a rare and expensive delicacy that is confined mostly to Japan. In 1999, wholesale prices for wasabi in Japan ranged from $25 to $85 per pound, and retail prices soared to more than $100. Even in Japan, a mere 5 percent of sushi shops can afford to use fresh wasabi. Only recently has real wasabi been made available in the U.S., thanks to growers like Pacific Farms in Oregon which charges about $25 for six 43-gram tubes (about a half-pound). It also sells wasabi plants for home gardening, but that is a difficult process.

THE PLANT AND A FAMILIAR FIRE SOURCE

There is a dispute over the botanical name of wasabi, with some sources giving *Eutrema wasabi* and others *Wasabia japonica*. It is a perennial herb native to Japan and eastern Siberia. The name is said to mean "mountain hollyhock." Its most pungent part, like that of ginger, is a rhizome. Like horseradish, it is cruciferous, related to mustard and cabbage; it grows about 2 feet tall. Its pungency comes from allyl isothiocyanate, the same pungent chemical found in horseradish and black mustard. Cultivated varieties of wasabi include "Daruma," the most popular, and "Mazuma," which has more heat.

Wasabi grows naturally in or near cold, shaded mountain streams with just the right mineral balance. It has been cultivated in Japan since the tenth century but is notoriously difficult to grow. Outdoor-cultivated wasabi plants require a constant supply of cool, running water, a loose gravel bed, and shade from trees or cloth to protect their leaves from sunburn.

In Japan, growers have learned to construct wasabi beds up to 3 feet deep using graduated sizes of gravel placed alongside cold streams and precisely arranged so water runs through them in a uniform pattern. The last beds in Japan, however, were reportedly built more than two hundred years ago. The highest quality wasabi is bed-grown and called *sawa* wasabi; when the plant is grown in fields, it is called *oka* wasabi and is generally considered inferior in terms of appearance and flavor. Wasabi requires cool conditions to grow, an ambient air temperature between 48 and 64 degrees. It can be grown from seed or from rhizome offshoots, and requires eighteen months or more to mature. It is now being grown in semi-aquatic conditions in greenhouses in British Columbia and in straight compost under shading in Seattle. There, the plants are misted twice daily. It is also cultivated on the coast of Oregon by Pacific Farms. There, it is grown in a recirculating, fully automatic hydroponic system in greenhouses, where the growers can harvest and replant every week of the year. There is commercial cultivation in raised beds in streams in New Zealand, and New Zealand Wasabi Ltd. has produced about ten tons per acre.

Wasabi also can be grown in pots or in the garden under shade netting but only if you live in a cool, moist climate. The growing wasabi plants must be kept moist, and that requires constant misting. Wasabi can also be grown in an air conditioned greenhouse.

The wasabi harvest usually occurs in the spring after the plants have established a new set of bright green leaves. The harvested rhizomes with the roots removed resemble knobby, thin, elongated pineapples.

WASABI IN THE KITCHEN

Wasabi has considerable amounts of potassium, calcium, and vitamin C. But since it is consumed in such small quantities, it is not a significant source of these nutrients. It contains cancer-fighting isothiocynates, and studies in Japan have indicated that wasabi is effective against stomach cancer cells. It is also thought to be antibacterial—a reason it is eaten with raw fish: to prevent food poisoning. And it has antifungal properties, too.

FORMS OF WASABI

The raw rhizomes, which can range from a couple of inches to nearly a foot in length, are sold in markets in Japan in pans of water; then they are grated into a fine paste with a pale green color. Choose only rhizomes that are not shriveled. Trim off any dark edges before grating, and scrub with a brush. Traditionally, a sharkskin grater, or *oroshi*, is used. If one is not available, a ceramic grater with very fine teeth is preferred over a stainless steel grater, but the latter can be used. Once the wasabi rhizome is grated, it is rinsed under cool water, drained, formed into a ball, and allowed to stand at room temperature for at least five minutes for the flavors to fully form. It should be consumed within twenty minutes, or all the pungency may dissipate.

Most of the "wasabi" paste is imitation—horseradish and Chinese mustard mixed with green food coloring. A true wasabi paste is produced by Pacific Farms. "Wasabi powder" from Japan is an imitation.

In Asian markets, wasabi is sometimes available in pickled form: the leaves, flowers, stalks, and rhizomes are chopped, brined, and mixed with sake, mirin, and sugar. In Japan, a wasabi wine and a wasabi liqueur are produced as well. Four wasabi salad dressings are made by Pacific Farms.

STORAGE

Wrapped in damp paper towels in the refrigerator, wasabi rhizomes will last about a month. Rinse in cold water once a week.

CULINARY USES

Freshly grated wasabi is mixed with soy sauce and used as a dip with sushi and sashimi. It is also added to soups and noodle dishes in Japan. American growers have used wasabi in drinks, appetizers like pâté, dips, sauces, salads, and seafood and meat entrees.

Horseradish and Wasabi Recipes

PREPARED HORSERADISH

This is the basic recipe for grated horseradish; it will retain its heat for about two weeks in the refrigerator because of the addition of the vinegar. Be sure to work in a well-ventilated kitchen, or the fumes will drive you out the door. Store the horseradish in a tightly sealed glass jar, but if you let the metal lid touch the horseradish, it will start to corrode the top.

> 1 piece fresh horseradish root, 4-ounces,
>   peeled and grated
> 2 tablespoons cider vinegar
> 1 tablespoon sugar
> 2 teaspoons salt

Combine all the ingredients in a bowl, and stir to blend. Store the mixture in a glass jar in the refrigerator.
Yield: 1 cup   **Heat scale:** Varies but usually medium-hot

CREAMY HORSERADISH SAUCE

Horseradish sauce is a classic condiment that's served with roast meats, beef in particular, and cooked or raw vegetables. Since horseradish is very volatile and loses its flavor and aroma quickly, this simple sauce should be made close to serving time. For an added hit of heat, we sometimes add ground habanero chile.

2/3 cup sour cream
1/4 cup fresh or Prepared Horseradish, commercial or
    see recipe on facing page
2 green onions, finely chopped
1 teaspoon distilled white vinegar
1 teaspoon sugar
3/4 teaspoon chopped fresh dill weed

Combine all the ingredients in a bowl, and beat until well mixed. Let the mixture sit for fifteen to twenty minutes to blend the flavors.

Yield: 2/3 cup   **Heat scale:** Medium

Wasabi Sauce for Beef or Fish

Using Japanese wasabi, this recipe is a remake of a classic early English horseradish sauce. It is perfect for rare roast beef or steak, smoked salmon, and any fried or baked fish dish. Make it just before you are ready to serve the meal to retain the full potency.

1 tablespoon white wine vinegar

1 teaspoon dry mustard

1/2 teaspoon lemon juice, fresh preferred

1/4 teaspoon sugar

1/4 teaspoon salt

Freshly ground black pepper

1/2 cup plus 2 tablespoons heavy cream, chilled

2 tablespoons wasabi paste

Combine the vinegar, mustard, lemon juice, sugar, salt, and black pepper in a small bowl, and whisk to form a smooth paste.

In another chilled bowl, whip the cream until it forms peaks. Add the whipped cream and wasabi to the mustard paste, stirring gently to blend.

Serve immediately.

Yield: 3/4 cup   **Heat scale:** Medium

HORSERADISH "PÂTÉ"

Here's a recipe for lovers of both bacon and horseradish. Serve the "pâté" over toast points or crackers of choice. It can also be used as a sandwich spread with combinations of different meats and cheeses.

    1 pound bacon
    2 medium white onions, minced (reserve 2 tablespoons)
    1/4 cup of prepared horseradish
        (reserve 1/2 tablespoon)
    1 clove of garlic, minced
    4 ounces Braunschweiger
    1 8-ounce block cream cheese

Fry the bacon in a large skillet, and then remove it to a plate to cool. Drain the excess grease from the skillet.

Add the minced onion and garlic to the skillet, and cook until softened.

Crumble the bacon, and add it to a mixing bowl. Add the onion, garlic, cream cheese, Braunschweiger, and horseradish (remember to reserve 1/2 tablespoon horseradish) to the bowl. Transfer the mixture to a serving dish.

Sprinkle the pâté with the reserved horseradish and onion. Serve with crackers.

Yield: About 3 cups   **Heat:** Medium

Wasabi Oyster Po' Boy Sandwiches

Now that you've made the wasabi mayonnaise, why not make some wasabi po' boy sandwiches that'll take your breath away? The following recipe makes four servings.

Wasabi Tartar Sauce:
1 cup wasabi mayonnaise

1/4 cup sweet pickle relish

2 tablespoons minced shallot or onion

2 tablespoons Dijon mustard

2 tablespoons minced fresh parsley leaves

1 teaspoon fresh lemon juice

1/4 teaspoon Louisiana-style hot sauce

Sandwich Filling:
Vegetable oil

2 loaves French bread

Butter or margarine

Cornmeal seasoned with black pepper and cayenne

24 shucked oysters, drained

Sliced tomatoes

Shredded lettuce

Heat the oil to 375 degrees in a deep fryer or heavy skillet.

Meanwhile, prepare the wasabi tartar sauce by stirring all the ingredients together in a small bowl and setting aside.

Slice the loaves of bread in half horizontally and vertically. Spread the inside surfaces with butter, then place the bread on a baking sheet, cut sides up. Heat the bread under a broiler for two or three minutes, or until lightly browned; set aside.

Place cornmeal mixture in a plastic bag. Drop in six oysters at a time and shake until they are well coated with cornmeal, then knock off the excess. Fry the oysters in batches of six or fewer, turning occasionally, until they're just cooked through and are golden brown, about a minute and a half. Drain on paper towels.

Spread 2 tablespoons of wasabi tartar sauce on each piece of bread. Arrange the oysters, tomatoes, and lettuce on the bottom slices of bread. Top with the remaining bread, and gently press together. Enjoy.

Yield: 4 servings   **Heat scale:** Mild

HORSERADISH SOUP WITH
TOASTED PUMPERNICKEL CROUTONS

In many of the Slavic countries, variations of horseradish soup are served as traditional Easter fare. Many of these soups are prepared with root vegetables such as beets, turnips, and, like this one, potatoes and a heavy dose of horseradish. This simple, hearty soup is easy to prepare and warms from the inside out. If you are watching your fat intake, substitute smoked turkey for the sausage.

    2 tablespoons butter or margarine, or
        substitute vegetable oil
    1/4 cup fresh breadcrumbs
    3 tablespoon chopped shallots
    1 quart vegetable or chicken broth
    2 cups russet potatoes, peeled and cubed
    1 cup grated horseradish, or substitute
        Prepared Horseradish, commercial, or see recipe,
        page 32
    1 cup cubed Polish sausage
    Salt and freshly ground black pepper to taste

CROUTONS:
    4 pumpernickel slices, crusts removed, cut into cubes
    2 tablespoons olive oil
    2 teaspoons ground paprika

To make the croutons, preheat the oven to 325 degrees. Place the bread on a sheet pan, and bake in the oven until toasted, turning once—about ten minutes. Heat a small saucepan over low heat, and add the oil and paprika. Simmer for five minutes to blend. Combine the oil mixture with the bread in a bowl and toss to coat. Spread the croutons back on the baking sheet, return to the oven, and bake for ten minutes or until crisp.

Heat a heavy saucepan or stock pot over medium heat, add the butter, and when melted, add the breadcrumbs and shallots. Saute for one minute to soften the shallots, but don't brown the crumbs.

Add the broth, potatoes, and horseradish, and bring to a boil. Reduce the heat, cover, and simmer until the potatoes and horse-radish are very tender, about forty-five minutes.

Place the soup in a blender or food processor, and process until smooth. Return the soup to the stock pot, and season to taste with the salt and pepper.

Heat a heavy skillet over medium-high heat, add the sausage, and saute until it is browned, about five minutes.

Bring the soup to a simmer, thinning with more broth if necessary.

To serve, ladle the soup into individual bowls, and garnish with the croutons.

Yield: 4 to 6 servings   **Heat scale:** Medium

ZHUA CHAO YU
(FRIED GINGER PRAWNS)

Deep-fried Chinese food is not heavy since cornstarch, rather than flour, is used as a coating. This not only produces a light crust that lets the shrimp flavor come through but also protects the shrimp from being overcooked. Although the dish is simple, the flavors are complex. The tartness of the lemon is tempered by the spice of the ginger, and both complement the flavor of the shrimp. This very-easy-to-prepare dish can be served as an entree, appetizer, or just one of a number of dishes on a Chinese banquet table.

3/4 cup cornstarch
12 ounces prawns or shrimp, peeled and deveined
Vegetable oil for frying, peanut preferred
3 tablespoons grated ginger
2 tablespoons chopped green onion
2 cups cooked white rice
Garnish of lemon slices

SAUCE:
2 teaspoons light soy sauce
1 tablespoon Chinese black vinegar
1 tablespoon rice wine or dry sherry
1 teaspoon sugar
1/2 teaspoon dark sesame oil
Salt and white pepper

Combine all the ingredients for the sauce in a small bowl, and stir to mix.

In another bowl, combine the cornstarch with enough water to make a thin paste. Add the prawns, and turn to coat.

Heat a wok or heavy skillet over medium-high heat, pour in the oil to a depth of a couple inches, and when hot, add the prawns and stir-fry until they are just golden, about a minute and a half. Remove and drain on paper towels. Pour off all but 1 tablespoon of the oil from the wok.

Add the onions and ginger to the wok, and stir-fry for forty-five seconds. Add the sauce, and bring to a boil. Return the prawns to the wok, and turn carefully in the sauce until it has been completely absorbed into the shrimp, only a minute.

Place the shrimp on a serving platter accompanied by the rice.

Yield: 4 servings   **Heat scale:** Mild

WASABI MAYONNAISE

Wasabi mayo is delicious on grilled salmon, salmon cakes, grilled tuna, or deep-fried oysters (and most any other seafood). Try perking up anything that uses mayonnaise, such as deviled eggs, tuna salad sandwiches, or the po' boy sandwiches below. This mayo recipe eliminates today's problems with raw eggs and possible salmonella because the egg base is heated before being emulsified into mayonnaise.

> 2 large egg yolks
> 2 tablespoons fresh lemon juice
> 2 tablespoons water
> 1/2 teaspoon sugar
> 1 teaspoon dry mustard
> 1 teaspoon salt
> 1 cup vegetable oil
> 1 tablespoons prepared wasabi paste

Have a bowl of cold water handy. Place the egg yolks, lemon juice, water, and sugar in a small pan, and heat over very low heat, stirring constantly. If the mixture starts to thicken, remove it from the heat immediately, but continue stirring. Dip the bottom of the pan into the cold water to stop the mixture from cooking.

Scrape the mixture into a blender, and let it cool for at least five minutes. Add the dry mustard and salt. Cover the blender, and turn it on. With the blender running, slowly drizzle the oil in a very thin stream, letting the blender emulsify the sauce. Stop the blender, and add the wasabi. Pulse or blend the mayonnaise just long enough to thoroughly incorporate the wasabi. Refrigerated, this mayonnaise should keep for at least a week.

Yield: 1½ cups   **Heat scale:** Medium but dissipates quickly

Horseradish Potato Salad

Here is a hearty potato salad that just begs to accompany a grilled steak. Years ago, we figured out what made the *kartoffelsalat* in Germany so tangy and tasty; the secret is to douse the hot potatoes with vinegar before cooling. We like the taste of apple cider vinegar, but white vinegar works well also. Vary the amount of horseradish to suit your tastes.

> 3 to 4 medium russet potatoes, peeled and cut in
>   3/4-inch cubes
> 2 to 3 tablespoons cider vinegar
> 1/2 cup mayonnaise
> 1/4 cup sour cream
> 2 to 3 tablespoons Prepared Horseradish sauce,
>   commercial or see recipe, page 32
>
> 1/4 cup minced dill or 2 to 3 teaspoons dried dill weed
> 1/4 cup finely chopped celery
> 2 tablespoons finely chopped green or red onion
> 2 tablespoons finely chopped fresh flat-leaf parsley
> 1 tablespoon finely chopped chives
> Salt and ground white pepper to taste.

In a saucepan or pressure cooker, cook the potatoes until done. Remove from the heat, drain, and place in a bowl. Sprinkle the vinegar over the potatoes, and gently toss to mix. Let the potatoes cool at room temperature.

Combine the mayonnaise, sour cream, horseradish, and dill. Taste, and adjust the seasonings. Cover, and chill in the refrigerator.

To serve, add the celery, onion, parsley, and chives to the potatoes, and gently toss to mix. Pour the dressing over the top, and gently toss again to mix. Season with salt and pepper, and serve.

Yield: 4 servings **Heat scale:** Mild to medium

PART 2

Pods: Chile Peppers and Their Condiments

NOMENCLATURE

Treatises have been written about the etymology of the various words used to describe the *Capsicums*: pepper, chile, chili, chilli, and chile pepper, chili pepper, and chilli pepper. Pepper, of course, is derived from the early confusion with the genus *Piper*, or black pepper, while chilli, chile, and chili are, in order, the Nahuatl (Aztec), Spanish, and American English spellings. Yes, our preferred term, "chile pepper" is redundant and uses the Spanish spelling, but at least it cannot be confused with chili con carne or black pepper.

THE PLANT AND ITS POWER

Chile peppers are perennial subshrubs, native to South America, which are grown as annuals in colder climates. They are a part of the large nightshade family, or Solanaceae, and are closely related to tomatoes, potatoes, tobacco, and eggplants. They are not related to black pepper, *Piper nigrum*.

The chile pepper genus is *Capsicum*, from the Greek *kapto*, meaning, appropriately enough, "to bite." The five domesticated species are:

- *Annuum,* meaning annual, which is an incorrect designation, as chile peppers are perennials. It includes most of the commonest varieties, such as New Mexican, jalapeño, bell, and wax.
- *Baccatum,* meaning berry-like. It consists of the South American peppers commonly known as *ajís*.
- *Chinense,* meaning from China, is also an incorrect designation since the species originated in the Amazon Basin. It includes the extremely hot habaneros.
- *Frutescens,* meaning "shrubby" or "brushy." It includes the familiar tabascos.

- **Pubescens,** meaning hairy. It includes the South American *rocotos* and the Mexican *manzanos*.

The active principle that causes heat in chile peppers is a crystalline alkaloid generically called capsaicin. It is produced by glands at the junction of the placenta and the pod wall. The capsaicin spreads unevenly throughout the inside of the pod, concentrated mostly in the placental tissue that holds the seeds.

Capsaicin is an incredibly powerful and stable alkaloid, seemingly unaffected by cold or heat, which retains its original potency despite time, cooking, or freezing. Because it has no flavor, color, or odor, the precise amount of capsaicin present in chiles can be measured only by a specialized laboratory procedure known as high performance liquid chromatography. Despite its lack of odor or flavor, it is one of the most pungent compounds known, detectable to the palate in dilutions of one to several million. It is slightly soluble in water but very soluble in alcohols, fats, and oils.

And by the way, if you are worried about capsaicin destroying your 5,000 to 10,000 taste buds, you should know that all of them are replaced every two weeks anyway. So forget about your taste buds, and concentrate on the binding of your lipid molecules!

THE MOST POPULAR SPICE—OR SPICY FOOD?

Of all the spicy ingredients in this book, chile peppers are the most widely cultivated commercially, and are grown in nearly every tropical and temperate country in the world. There is quite a debate over whether chiles or black pepper are the most traded and popular spice, since the answer is difficult to determine. The reason is that black pepper is grown only as a spice, but chile peppers are grown as a spice when powdered, as a food when used as a vegetable, and as a major ingredient in prepared foods.

Statistics give us the answer: In 2002, worldwide black pepper production was about 321,000 metric tons, while in 1986 in India alone, chile pepper production was about 708,000 tons. Black pepper may be the most widely used spice around the world, but there is no question that chile pepper production—and use in cuisine—outweighs that of black pepper by a factor of at least eight. India is the largest producer of dried chile peppers, followed by Mexico, Indonesia, China, South Korea, Thailand, Ethiopia, the U.S., Taiwan, and Malaysia. Virtually no black pepper is grown by home gardeners, but tons of chile peppers are.

CHILES IN THE CLINIC AND THE KITCHEN

Most of the research on the nutritional properties of hot peppers has concerned the New Mexican pod types because they are consumed more as a food than a condiment. The long green pods are harvested, roasted and peeled, and then are stuffed or made into sauces. Some of the green pods are allowed to turn red on the bush; after harvesting, these are used as the primary ingredient in red chile sauces. The green chiles are quite high in vitamin C, with about twice the amount as citrus by weight, while dried red chiles contain more vitamin A than carrots. Vitamin C is one of the least stable of all the vitamins; it is broken down chemically by heat, exposure to air, solubility in water, and dehydration. Vitamin A, however, is one of the most stable vitamins and is not affected by canning, cooking, or time.

A high percentage of vitamin C in fresh green chiles is retained in the canned and frozen products, but the vitamin C content drops dramatically in the dried red pods and powder. Each hundred grams of fresh ripe chile pods contains 369 milligrams of vitamin C, which diminishes by more than half to 154 milligrams in the dried red pods. Red chile powder contains less than 3 percent of the vitamin C of ripe pods, a low 10 milligrams.

The amount of vitamin A increases dramatically as the pod turns red and dries, from 770 units per hundred grams of green pods to 77,000 in freshly processed dried red pods. This hundred-fold rise in vitamin A content is the result of increasing carotene, the chemical that produces the orange and red colors of ripe peppers. The recommended daily allowances for these vitamins are 5,000 International Units for A and 60 milligrams for C. These can be satisfied by eating about a teaspoonful of red chile sauce for A and an ounce of fresh green chile for C.

Each hundred grams of green chile contains less than two-tenths of a gram of fat—a very low amount. Since no cholesterol is found in vegetable products, peppers are free of it. The fiber content of fresh hot peppers is fairly high (between 1.3 and 2.3 grams per hundred grams of chile), and many of the dishes prepared with them use starchy ingredients such as beans, pasta, and tortillas. The sugar of chiles is in the form of healthy complex carbohydrates.

Fresh green chile contains only 3.5 to 5.7 milligrams of sodium per hundred grams—a very low amount.

FORMS

Literally hundreds of varieties of peppers are grown in the world, but only a dozen or two are used for cooking in the U.S. The following survey is not intended to be exhaustive but rather is a general description of the most popular peppers in the United States.

Fresh peppers, available from the garden or the market, are becoming increasingly popular as they become more commonly available. The most ubiquitous peppers are, of course, the familiar bells, which have no heat except for a variety called "Mexi-Bell," with a mild bite. The poblano, similar in size to a bell, is a Mexican pepper with moderate to mild heat; it is often stuffed with cheese and baked.

The most readily available hot peppers in the produce sections of supermarkets are jalapeños and yellow wax peppers. The yellow wax peppers are usually mild, and are stuffed or chopped for use in salsas and salads. Jalapeños and serranos—either green or fresh red—are used in a similar manner, and are often floated whole in soups or stews to provide a little extra bite, then are removed before serving. Another variety that sometimes appears fresh is the cherry pepper. This mild pepper is often pickled.

Several varieties of the long green New Mexican chiles are available fresh in the Southwest and occasionally in other locations. The "NuMex 6-4 Heritage" variety is the most commonly grown, and is available from August through early November. Its hotter cousin, "Sandia," is usually not seen in the green, or immature, form. The mildest New Mexican-type variety is the "Anaheim," a California pepper that is available most of the year. Occasionally, New Mexican chiles are identified by their grower (such as Barker) or by a regional appellation (Chimayó, Hatch, or Luna County), which further confuses the issue.

All of these long green chiles must be roasted and peeled before being used in a recipe. Blistering or roasting the chile is the process of heating it until the tough transparent skin is separated from the meat so it can be removed. The method is quite simple.

While processing the chiles, be sure to wear rubber gloves to protect yourself from the capsaicin, which can burn your hands and any other part of your body that you touch. Before roasting, cut a small slit in each chile close to the top to let the steam escape. The chiles can then be placed on a baking sheet and put directly under the broiler or on a screen on top of the stove.

My favorite method is to place the pods on a charcoal grill about 5 to 6 inches from the coals. Blisters will soon indicate that the skin is separating, but be sure the chiles are blistered all over or they will not peel properly. Immediately wrap them in damp towels or place them in a plastic bag for ten to fifteen minutes— this "steams" them and loosens the skins. For crisper, less-cooked chiles, plunge them into ice water to stop the cooking process.

I find that freezing is the most flavorful method of preservation. If the pods are to be frozen whole (rather than chopped), they do not have to be peeled first. In fact, they are easier to peel after they have been frozen. After roasting the chiles, freeze them in the form in which you plan to use them—whole, strips, or chopped. If you are storing them in strips or chopped, peel the pods first. A handy way to put up chopped or diced chiles is to freeze them in ice cube trays with sections. When frozen, they can be popped out of the trays and stored in a bag in the freezer. Just drop in a cube when you're making a soup or stew! This eliminates the problems inherent in hacking apart a large slab of frozen chiles when you need just a couple of ounces. New Mexican chiles are available fresh in season by overnight delivery. They are found canned in most U.S. markets and frozen in some parts of the Southwest.

Other fresh chiles that are sometimes found in markets (especially farmers' markets) are serranos and habaneros. The serranos—smaller, thinner, and hotter than jalapeños—are the classic chiles of the Mexican pico de gallo fresh salsas. Habaneros, the world's hottest peppers, are lantern-shaped orange or red devils that have a unique, fruity aroma in addition to their powerful punch. Use them with caution.

Generally speaking, any of the small fresh peppers may be substituted for another; however, they are not a substitute for poblanos or the New Mexican varieties in recipes. The smaller chiles—habaneros, serranos, and jalapeños—can be frozen without processing. Wash the chiles, dry them, place them one layer deep on a cookie sheet, and freeze them. After they are frozen solid, store them in a bag. Frozen chiles will keep for nine months to a year at zero degrees. All the small peppers can be frozen whole with no further processing needed, and their texture holds up surprisingly well in the freezer.

Like fresh peppers, the larger dried chiles are, the milder. The large dried peppers, such as ancho (a dried poblano) and the New Mexican varieties, are mild enough to be the principal ingredients of sauces. The smaller varieties, such as piquin, are too hot for this purpose and are generally used as condiments or in stir-frying. All dried peppers can be ground into powders. (See Part 4 of this book.)

Four large peppers are mainly used as the base for sauces: ancho, pasilla, New Mexican, and guajillo. The ancho is a wide, dark pepper with a "raisiny" aroma. It is the only pepper that is commonly stuffed in its dried form. (The pod is softened in water first.) The pasilla is a long, thin, dark pepper that also has a raisiny or nutty aroma. Along with the ancho, it commonly appears in Mexican *mole* sauces.

The most common way to use the red New Mexican chiles is to hang them in long strings, or ristras, until they are ready to be used in cooking. Then they are commonly rehydrated and combined with onions, garlic, oil, spices, and water to make the classic New Mexican red chile sauce, a common topping for enchiladas in the Southwest. The guajillos, a shortened and hotter version of the New Mexican chiles, are commonly used in sauces in northern Mexico.

There are a bewildering number of small, hot pods ranging in size from that of a little fingernail (the chiltepín) to the skinny 6-inch cayenne. Some varieties include piquin, Thai, santaka, de árbol, mirasol, and tabasco. These chiles appear in stir-fry dishes, are floated in soups or stews, or are used to add heat to sauces that are too mild. A specialized dried chile that has become quite popular is the chipotle, a smoke-dried red jalapeño.

PREPARED CHILE PRODUCTS

There are more varieties of manufactured chile products than any other spicy ingredient in this book—proof of chile's incredible diversity:

- **Barbecue sauce,** by type of chile, including chipotle, habanero, jalapeño, serrano; by country, including African, Asian, U.S.;
- **Cheeses;**
- **Condiments,** including chile oil, horseradish, ketchup, meat sauce (cocktail, poultry, steak);

- **Drinks and drink mixes;**
- **Dry mixes** (enchilada sauces, etc.);
- **Grilling sauces;**
- **Hot sauce,** including Caribbean-style, fruit, habanero, Louisiana-style, specialty chile (chipotle, jalapeño, serrano, other), wing sauce, and world beat (African, Asian);
- **Meats,** including sausages and ribs;
- **Mustards;**
- **Olives;**
- **Pasta sauces;**
- **Pickled products;**
- **Prepared dips;**
- **Prepared sauces** (red chile, green chile, enchilada);
- **Relishes;**
- **Salad dressings;**
- **Salsa,** including chipotle, fruit, habanero, tomatillo;
- **Snacks,** including chips, crackers, jerky, nuts, pretzels, snack mixes;
- **Soups and stews,** including chili con carne;
- **Spice blends,** including curry powders and meat rubs, jerk seasoning, dry salsa mixes;
- **Sweet and hot sauces** (hot fudge, glazes);
- **Sweet heat** (candy, cakes/pastries, cookies, jams/jellies);
- **Table seasonings;**
- **Vinegars.**

MAKING ESSENTIAL CHILE INGREDIENTS AND CONDIMENTS

Please note that hot sauces, including salsas, have their own book in this series, so they are not covered here.

Asian Chile Paste

Popular throughout Southeast Asia, this garlic and chile-based paste is used as a condiment that adds fire without greatly altering the taste of the dish. It is especially good for stir-frys. This is a great recipe for using up any small chiles that are left at the end of the season. The paste will keep for up to three months in the refrigerator, and it can also be frozen.

> 1 cup small fresh red chiles, stems removed, such as
>   Thai, serrano, piquin, or japones
> 1/3 cup distilled white vinegar
> 8 cloves garlic, chopped
> 3 tablespoons vegetable oil
> 1 teaspoon salt
> Water as needed

Place all the ingredients in a blender or food processor, and purée, adding water if necessary, to form a thick paste.

Yield: 1 cup   **Heat scale:** Hot

CHILE VINEGAR

This is my favorite vinegar. Recommended chiles include serranos and habaneros, but it can also be made with dried pasillas for a raisiny flavor. Note: This recipe requires advance preparation.

2 tablespoons minced fresh small chiles
1 cup fresh rosemary leaves
3 cloves garlic
1 quart white vinegar

In a large jar, cover the chiles, rosemary, and garlic with the vinegar, and replace the lid tightly. Place the jar in a cool, dark place, and leave the bottles undisturbed for three to four weeks. Strain, pour into clean, sterilized bottles, and label them.

Yield: 1 quart   **Heat scale:** Varies

PIRI PIRI OIL

This interesting condiment is the Caribbean oil-based variation on the African sauce from Angola, which was transferred to the region by Portuguese immigrants working the cacao plantations in Trinidad and Guyana. Use it to spice up soups and fried fish. Pimento leaves are traditionally used in this recipe, but they are hard to find. Note: The recipe requires advance preparation.

    3 cups extra virgin olive oil
    2 habanero chiles, cut in half
    1 teaspoon lemon zest
    2 bay leaves

Combine all ingredients in a jar, and seal tightly. Place in the refrigerator, and let steep for two weeks. Remove the top and stir every two or three days. The longer it steeps, the hotter the oil will become.

Yield: 3 cups   **Heat scale:** Hot

CHIPOTLES ADOBADOS (CHIPOTLE CHILES IN ADOBO SAUCE)

Here's a recipe from Tlaxcala, Mexico. These sweet-hot pickled chiles can be the basis of a sauce of their own if they're further puréed, or can be served as a condiment with enchiladas and other main dishes.

1/2 pound dried chipotle chiles, stems removed
Water to rehydrate
1 quart vinegar
1 head garlic, peeled and crushed
1/2 cup piloncillo, or 1/2 cup packed brown sugar
1 cup roasted and peeled green chile, such as
poblano or New Mexican
2 medium tomatoes, chopped
6 black peppercorns
3 bay leaves
1 teaspoon ground cumin
Salt to taste

Soak the chipotles in water until they rehydrate, at least an hour, then drain.

In a saucepan, add 1/2 the vinegar, 1/2 the garlic, and the brown sugar. Cook this mixture for about twenty minutes, then add the chipotles.

In another pan, combine the green chile, tomato, remaining garlic, peppercorns, bay leaves, cumin, remaining vinegar, and salt to taste. Cook covered for about thirty minutes over medium heat. Add the chipotle chile mixture, stir well, and store in sterilized jars.

Yield: About 1½ quarts   **Heat scale:** Hot

THE EARLIEST *MOLE* SAUCE

Why wouldn't the cooks of the prehistoric, ash-covered village of Cerén have developed sauces to serve over meats and vegetables? After all, there is evidence that curry mixtures existed thousands of years ago in what is now India, and we have to assume that Native Americans experimented with all available ingredients. Since both chiles and chocolate were found together during the archaeological excavation of the village, perhaps this *mole* sauce was served over stewed duck meat, as ducks were one of the domesticated meat sources of the Cerén villagers.

> 3 tablespoons pumpkin or squash seeds (pepitas)
> 4 tomatillos, husks removed
> 1 tomato, roasted and peeled
> 1/2 teaspoon chile seeds, from dried chile pods
> 1 corn tortilla, torn into pieces
> 2 tablespoons red chile powder, such as New Mexican,
>   guajillo, or Chimayó
> 1 teaspoon annatto seeds, or substitute achiote paste
> 3 tablespoons vegetable oil
> 2½ cups chicken broth
> 1 ounce Mexican chocolate, or substitute
>   bittersweet chocolate

Heat a heavy skillet over high heat, add the pumpkin seeds, and dry roast until the seeds start to pop. Shake the skillet once they start to pop until they turn golden, about three to five minutes. Be sure that they don't darken, and remove from the pan to cool completely. Place the seeds in a spice mill or coffee grinder, and process to a fine powder.

Put the seeds, tomatillos, tomato, chile seeds, tortilla, chile powder, and achiote in a blender or food processor, and process with just enough broth to form a paste.

Reheat the skillet over medium heat, add the oil, and add the paste when it is hot. Fry the paste, stirring constantly, until it is fragrant, about four minutes.

Whisk in the remaining chicken broth and the chocolate, and cook, stirring constantly, until thickened to the desired consistency. If the sauce becomes too thick, thin with either broth or water.

Yield: 2 cups   **Heat scale:** Medium

Sambal Oelek
(Hot Chile and Lime Condiment)

Sambals are multipurpose condiments that are popular throughout Indonesia, Malaysia, and India with multitude of variations. This basic, hot sambal, which has been called the "mother" of all the Indonesian sambals, is also spelled "olek" or "ulek." Since "oelek" means hot peppers, we'll go with that spelling. This sambal goes well with meats and poultry and is also a perfect condiment for just adding heat to your meal. It can also be used as a base for creating other sambals or as a substitute for fresh chile peppers in recipes.

1 cup dried red chiles, such as piquins or cayennes, stems removed
6 cloves garlic
3 tablespoons lime juice, fresh preferred
1 tablespoon vegetable oil, peanut preferred

Place the chiles in a bowl, cover with hot water, and let them steep for fifteen minutes to soften. Remove the chiles, drain, and discard the water.

Combine all the ingredients in a blender or food processor, and purée until smooth. Thin the sambal with more lime juice if desired.

Yield: 1/3 to 1/2 cup   **Heat scale:** Extremely hot

PART 3

Seeds: Mustard and All Kinds of Pepper

Mustard

It figures that the first contact with mustard for most of us is its use as a condiment for hot dogs—perhaps its most common purpose. But there's a lot more to mustard than hot dogs; it's a versatile spice that is combined at some point in cooking with every other spicy ingredient featured in this book.

The word mustard comes from the medieval Latin term *mustum ardens*, meaning "burning wine must," because mustard preparations were made by crushing the seeds with unfermented grape must, or juice. That process resulted in releasing the pungent—or burning—qualities of the seeds. That Latin phrase then became the Old French *moustarde* which became the modern French *moutarde*—in English, mustard.

THE PLANT AND ITS POTENCY

As often occurs, scientists do not agree on the botanical names of the various species of mustard. White mustard, or *Brassica alba*, is often known as either *Sinapis alba* or *Brassica hirta*, while black mustard is known as *Brassica nigra*, and brown mustard is named *Brassica juncea*. Further confusing the issue are the common names given to these species. White mustard is also called yellow mustard because of the pale yellow color of the seeds, which are so tiny they can number 15,000 to an ounce. Brown mustard is sometimes called black mustard, but its seeds are dark red to brown, and black mustard is also known as Indian mustard, Chinese mustard, and mustard greens.

All mustards are annual plants living in temperate climates and often growing as weeds. White mustard grows to 6 feet tall in some areas and loves full sun. From sowing in the spring to harvesting takes only about two months, so it's a fast-growing plant. The most commonly cultivated mustards are the white and brown varieties. Black mustard grows too tall (up to 15 feet) and its seeds drop too easily for mechanical harvesting. Mustard is not usually cultivated in the home garden.

World production of mustard seed was 468,000 metric tons in 2002. The largest producer was Canada, with 154,000 metric tons; other countries with significant production were Nepal (134,000 m.t.), the United States (56,000 m.t.), the Czech Republic (32,213 m.t.), and Burma (Myanmar) with 30,024 metric tons. Mature mustard plants are harvested much like wheat. The "hay" is stacked in sheaves to dry and then threshed to remove the seeds.

The seeds of all mustards contain about 30 percent oil, which contains the pungent principles. The pungency of mustard occurs when a liquid such as water, wine, or vinegar is added to the ground seed, and an enzyme, myrosin, combines with a glycoside, sinigrin, to produce the sulfur compound allyl isothiocyanate. The reaction takes about ten to fifteen minutes. This is the identical pungent principle found in horseradish and wasabi. Black mustard is the most pungent of the three species, with brown next and white the least pungent. More important to the pungency is what is mixed with the ground seeds to make mustard paste. Water makes the hottest mustard, and vinegar tends to both temper the heat and prevent deterioration of the pungent oil. Wine produces a pungent, spicy flavor, and for some unknown reason, beer makes the hottest mustard.

MUSTARD IN THE KITCHEN AND CLINIC

Mustard contains between 28 and 36 percent protein as well as calcium, magnesium, potassium, and niacin. A gram of mustard flour (powder) has 4.3 calories, only trace amounts of fat, and no cholesterol. The heat of mustard does not linger but dissipates quickly and is said to stimulate the appetite. The essential oil retards growth of molds, yeasts, and bacteria.

It is used externally in bandages, plasters, and poultices for respiratory infections, arthritic joints, and skin eruptions. A mustard footbath is a traditional remedy for colds and headaches. In Chinese medicine, mustard is taken internally for bronchial congestion, coughs, and joint pains. Mustard plasters, made by adding water to mustard powder and spreading the mixture on a bandage, can be quite hot and irritate the skin, eventually causing blisters, so care should be taken and the plaster removed when it becomes uncomfortable

FORMS

Besides being crushed to make mustard pastes of all kinds, the uncrushed seeds are widely used in preserving such foods as sauerkraut, sausages, and pickles. Mustard powder, or flour, is produced by grinding together white and black mustard seeds and then sifting the mixture to remove the hull fragments. Wheat flower is added for bulk, turmeric for a bright yellow color, and also small amounts of sugar, salt, and spices. Because the hulls have been removed, this powder is quite pungent. Dry mustard is often flavored with hot spices such as chile powder or ground black pepper, or mild herbs such as basil, tarragon, thyme, cumin, or mint. Even fresh ingredients such as ginger or horseradish can be added. The powder can then be mixed with water, vinegar, ale, or cider to make an instant prepared mustard.

Commercially prepared mustards are pastes and are described in several ways. By country, we have American mustard, which uses only white mustard seeds; English, using a mixture of white and black seeds; German, using black or brown seeds; and French, which is based on brown mustard seeds. By pungency, there are strong mustards (mostly black, sometimes brown seeds) or mild mustards (white seeds or white and brown seeds). Two additional categories are whole-grain mustards and flavored mustards.

The type of seed used is only part of the pungency; mustards are made milder by leaving in a percentage of the less-pungent hulls. These are called whole grain mustards, and the most famous of them are the Dijon mustards. There are three types of French mustard: Bordeaux, which is mild and brown and often contains herbs such as tarragon; Dijon, which is stronger, pale yellow, and usually lacking in extra flavorings; and Meaux, which is mild because it is made with the unmilled, crushed seeds. Ninety percent of all French mustards made are the Dijon type. German mustard is of the Bordeaux type and is often flavored with herbs. Chinese mustard is simply mustard flour mixed with water.

Flavored mustards have additional herbs, spices, or other flavorings added, such as horseradish, chiles, lemon, peppercorns, mint, basil, tarragon, chives, ginger, and curry powder. Therefore, it is theoretically possible to create a mustard using every spicy ingredient in this book. Sweet mustards have sugar or honey added; the bright yellow color of some American-style prepared mustards comes from the addition of turmeric.

Mustard oil, 93 percent allyl isothiocyanate, is a polyunsaturated cooking oil that is pressed from the seeds of the brown and black varieties. Most mustard oil is manufactured in India. It loses its pungency when heated, but because of its high smoking point, it is used to stir-fry and deep-fry and is very popular in Indian cooking. If the oil is made in India or elsewhere in Asia, it might be black mustard oil, which must be heated to the smoking point before being used in cooking.

STORAGE

Store the seeds in airtight containers, preferably glass, in a cool, dry cupboard or spice rack.

Store dry mustard the same way. Store prepared mustards in airtight containers in the refrigerator. They will keep their strength for about a year. Store mustard oil in the refrigerator to slow the oxidation process.

CULINARY USES

Mustard seeds are commonly used whole in pickles and sausages, and are added to coleslaw, potato salad, and cooked cabbage and beets. Crushed, they are added to dips for seafood and to salad dressings. Other sauces and condiments, such as mayonnaise, vinaigrettes, and dill sauces have powdered or prepared mustard as an ingredient. Dry mustard is a preservative and is often added to pickles and chutneys. Mustard sauces are sprinkled over salads. Prepared mustards are served cold as condiments for cold meats or hot sandwiches like pastrami, or are added to hot dishes at the end of the cooking process. (Otherwise, the cooking will kill the mustard's pungency.) Mustard is often used in glazes for roasted meats, in sauces for ham or corned beef, and as a major ingredient in casseroles, salad dressings, and cocktail sauces.

CRACKED BLACK PEPPERCORN MUSTARD

This is a quick, easy-to-prepare mustard with a distinctive peppercorn flavor. Its assertive flavor is excellent on dark breads and smoked meats, and makes a perfect coating for steaks or burgers before grilling. Add a little of this mustard to beef gravy for an added flavor dimension. Note: This recipe requires advance preparation.

1/4 cup whole yellow mustard seeds
1/4 cup champagne vinegar
1/4 cup hot water
2 tablespoons coarsely cracked black peppercorns
1 teaspoon garlic powder
1/2 teaspoon salt

Place the mustard seeds in a spice mill or coffee grinder, and process until finely ground. Combine the mustard and vinegar in a bowl, and stir to mix. Let the mixture sit for fifteen minutes.

Place all the ingredients in a blender or food processor, and process until smooth. Spoon the mustard into a sterilized jar, cover, and refrigerate for one week before using.

Yield: 1/2 cup   **Heat scale:** Medium

DIJON-STYLE MUSTARD

The name "Dijon Moutarde" is strictly controlled by French law. It can be used only on mixtures that contain black and/or brown mustard seeds, which must be mixed with either wine, wine vinegar, or vertus—the juice of unripe grapes. Any product of milder, white seeds may be labeled "condiment" but never "moutarde." This is a wonderful mustard to use as a base for adding other ingredients such as fruits and herbs. The flavor changes from sharp to smooth and mellow, hence the long aging period. The proportions of ingredients used in the French Dijon Moutarde are a closely guarded secret, but this recipe is the closest we've come to the real McCoy. Note: The recipe requires advance preparation.

3/4 cup mustard powder
1 cup champagne vinegar
1 cup dry white wine
1/2 cup minced onions
2 tablespoons minced shallots
2 tablespoons minced garlic
2 bay leaves
20 black peppercorns
10 juniper berries
1/2 teaspoon dried tarragon
1/4 teaspoon dried thyme
3 tablespoons lemon juice, fresh preferred
2 teaspoons salt
2 teaspoons sugar

Combine the mustard powder with 1/4 cup cold water in a bowl, and stir to form a paste.

In a saucepan, combine the vinegar, wine, onion, shallots, garlic, peppercorns, juniper berries, tarragon, and thyme. Bring the mixture to a simmer over moderate heat, and cook until it is re-duced by two-thirds. Strain the mixture into a bowl, cover, and chill.

When cooled, stir the vinegar reduction into the mustard paste. Add the lemon juice, salt, and sugar, and stir to combine. Let the mixture stand for thirty minutes.

Transfer the mustard to a saucepan, and simmer over low heat for fifteen minutes. Remove the pan from the heat, and let it cool.

Spoon the mustard into a sterilized jar, and seal. Store the mustard in a dark, cool place for three weeks before using.

Yield: 1½ cups   **Heat scale:** Medium to hot

COARSE-GRAINED GERMAN-STYLE BEER MUSTARD

This is a full-flavored, coarse-textured mustard that's both mustard mild and robustly spicy from the cinnamon and allspice. It's a good accompaniment to sausages, wursts, and ham, as well as an addition to the dressing for German potato salad, or even a coating for roast beef. Other ingredients such as sun-dried tomatoes and chiles can be added to the basic recipe to enhance the mustard. Note: This recipe requires advance preparation.

> 1/2 cup yellow mustard seeds
> 1/3 cup brown mustard seeds
> 1/4 cup mustard powder
> 1 cup dark beer
> 1 cup cider vinegar
> 2 tablespoons brown sugar
> 4 whole cloves
> 1/2 teaspoon garlic powder
> 1/2 teaspoon caraway seeds
> 1/4 teaspoon ground cinnamon
> 1/4 teaspoon allspice
> 1/4 teaspoon mace

Place the yellow and brown mustard seeds in a spice grinder or coffee grinder, and pulse to process so they still remain coarse.

Combine all the mustards and the beer in a bowl, and let the mixture soak overnight.

Combine the vinegar, sugar, cloves, garlic powder, caraway, cinnamon, allspice, and mace in a nonreactive saucepan over medium heat. Simmer the mixture until it's reduced by half, about ten minutes. Cool, and strain into the mustard mix.

Cook the mustard in the top of a double boiler for five to ten minutes, stirring frequently, until it is slightly thickened. Remember that the mustard will thicken as it cools, so don't cook for too long.

Then let the mixture cool, spoon it into a sterilized jar, and refrigerate for three days before using.

Yield: 1½ to 2 cups   **Heat scale:** Mild

GINGER PLUM SAUCE MUSTARD

This mustard is both sweet and hot with a crisp, sharp, distinctive flavor. The sweetness comes from the ginger, plum sauce, and even the vinegar if Chinese vegetarian black vinegar is used. (This vinegar, which can be found in Asian markets, has a very distinctive, fruity, salty, complex, nonacidic taste.) This is a very easy mustard to prepare, and makes a great dipping sauce for Asian appetizers as well as a glaze on ham or duck. Note: This recipe requires advance preparation.

1/4 cup brown mustard seeds, finely ground
1/2 cup yellow mustard powder
2 tablespoons Chinese vegetarian black vinegar
    (available in Asian markets), or substitute rice or
    distilled white vinegar
3 tablespoons Chinese plum sauce (available in
    Asian markets)
1/3 cup grated ginger
1 tablespoon brown sugar
1 teaspoon finely minced garlic

Place the mustard seeds in a spice mill or coffee grinder, and process to a powder.

Combine the mustards, add the vinegar, plum sauce, and 1/4 cup water in a bowl, and stir to form a paste. Add the ginger, sugar, and garlic, and mix well.

Spoon the mustard into a sterilized jar, and refrigerate for one week before using.

Yield: 1 cup   **Heat scale:** Medium

CHIPOTLE LIME MUSTARD

This is a Southwest-inspired mustard that is slightly grainy, with a definite taste of cumin, and is milder than many mustards that don't contain chiles. It's good with just about anything: as a marinade for poultry, pork, or beef; mixed with sour cream or mayonnaise for a tasty dip; or as a topping for vegetables. Note: This recipe requires advance preparation.

1/2 cup yellow mustard seeds
1/2 cup mustard powder
1/4 cup chopped onion
2 teaspoons chopped garlic
1/3 cup cider vinegar
2 tablespoons lime juice, fresh preferred
2 chipotle chiles en adobo
2 to 4 tablespoons water
2 teaspoons cumin seeds
1 teaspoon salt

Place the mustard seeds in a spice mill or coffee grinder, and coarsely grind. Combine the ground mustard seeds, powder, and 1/2 cup cold water in a bowl, and stir to mix. Let sit for three hours.

Place the remaining ingredients in a blender or food processor, and process until smooth. Stir the mixture into the mustard.

Place the mixture in a saucepan, and bring to a boil over medium-high heat. Lower the heat, and simmer for five minutes or until the mixture thickens slightly, stirring occasionally and adding water to thin. Remember that the mustard will thicken as it cools, so don't cook it too long.

Spoon the mustard into a sterilized jar, and refrigerate for one week before using.

Yield: 1 to 1½ cups   **Heat scale:** Medium

CREOLE MUSTARD

This mustard is a specialty of Louisiana's German Creoles, and is a traditional flavoring in the cuisine of New Orleans. It's a must in the preparation of remoulade sauce. This is a sharp and slightly sweet mustard with a complex flavor. It will definitely clean out the sinuses. Quick and easy to prepare, it's a good accompaniment to shrimp, ham, fish, and poultry as well as an important flavor ingredient in many Cajun and Creole dishes. Note: This recipe requires advance preparation.

1/4 cup yellow mustard powder
1 tablespoon all-purpose flour
1 tablespoon Dijon-style commercial mustard
3 tablespoons white wine vinegar
2 teaspoons grated horseradish
1 clove garlic, minced
1 teaspoon sugar
1/2 teaspoon dried thyme
1/2 teaspoon paprika
1/2 teaspoon ground white pepper
1/4 teaspoon salt

Combine all the ingredients along with 1/2 cup water in a saucepan, and mix well. Heat to a simmer over medium heat, and cook for two minutes. Add more water if the mustard gets too thick. Remove the pan, and let the mustard cool.

Spoon it into a sterilized jar, and refrigerate for one week before using.

Yield: 1/2 cup   **Heat scale:** Medium

SWEET CORN CHOWDER WITH MUSTARD OF CHOICE

This mustardy recipe makes a sweet heat side dish that goes well with roasted meats. Feel free to add more mustard to really spice it up.

2 tablespoons butter

2 tablespoons flour

2 tablespoons mustard of choice from this book, or more to taste

2 cups chicken stock

2 cups canned sweet corn (measured after draining)

1/2 cup diced ham

1 green onion, finely chopped

2/3 cup heavy cream

Salt and pepper to taste

Melt the butter over low heat in a medium-size saucepan. Add the flour and mustard powder, and cook over low heat, stirring constantly, for one to two minutes. Gradually stir in the chicken stock (don't worry about lumps), then bring the mixture to a boil over medium heat, stirring continuously until it thickens.

Add the corn and ham. Cover, and cook for five to eight minutes, stirring frequently. Add the green onion and heavy cream, and continue cooking only until the mixture is thoroughly warmed. (Don't let it boil.) Serve immediately.

Yield: 4 servings   **Heat scale:** Mild to medium

Gravlax with Spicy Mustard Sauce

This Swedish dish takes two days to make, but it's well worth the effort. The Vikings in the eighth century are credited with developing gravlax as a way of preserving fish when they were out marauding, pillaging, and raiding. The name comes from the word "grav," which means grave, and "laxs," or salmon; since the fish was often buried in the cold ground to preserve it, the name is appropriate. The traditional way to serve gravlax is to slice it as thinly as possible, place it on black bread or toasted rye bread, and serve with a little mustard sauce spread over the top. Note: This recipe requires advance preparation.

1/4 cup sugar
1/3 cup kosher salt
1 tablespoon coarsely ground black pepper
2 small bunches dill, coarsely chopped
1 bunch flat-leaf parsley, chopped
1 bunch lemon balm, chopped
1/2 bunch chervil, chopped
2 salmon fillets, about 1½ pounds each

Mustard Sauce:
3 tablespoons vegetable oil
2 tablespoons Cracked Black Pepper Mustard,
   commercial or see recipe, page 67
2 tablespoons sugar
2 tablespoons distilled white vinegar
2 tablespoons freshly chopped dill
1 tablespoon mustard powder
1 tablespoon gin or aquavit (optional)

Combine the sugar, salt, and pepper in a bowl to make the sugar mixture. In another bowl, combine the dill, chervil, parsley, and lemon balm to make the herb mixture. In a third bowl, combine all the ingredients to make the mustard sauce, and stir to mix. Cover the bowl, and refrigerate.

Place one fillet skin side down in a shallow bowl. Sprinkle half the sugar mixture over it, then half of the herb mixture, the rest of the sugar mixture, and the rest of the herb mixture. Place the second fillet on top of the first, flesh to flesh, and cover with plastic wrap.

Place the wrapped fillets in a shallow pan, and weigh them down with something heavy, like a cast iron skillet with a couple of bricks in it. Refrigerate for twenty-four hours, then flip the fillets, weigh them down again, and refrigerate for another twenty-four hours.

To make the mustard sauce, combine all the ingredients in a bowl, and mix well.

Thinly slice the salmon, and serve with rye or black bread and the mustard sauce.

Yield: 12 or more servings   **Heat scale:** Mild

BAYOU SHRIMP AND WILTED SPINACH SALAD WITH TRIPLE MUSTARD DRESSING

Three types of mustard are used in this recipe. If you want to increase the spice level, add more of the dry mustard, as it will increase the pungency without altering the taste. Any type of loose leaf lettuce may be used in place of the spinach. Heating the dressing brings out the tangy flavor of the mustard. This is a great summer entree salad. Prepare the salad and dressing, grill the shrimp, and assemble the salad at the table. Note: This recipe requires advance preparation.

1 to 1½ pounds shrimp, shelled and deveined
2 to 2½ tablespoons commercial Creole seasoning or
  Cajun spice mix
2 teaspoons vegetable oil
10-ounce package baby spinach, or
  1 bunch spinach rinsed and torn into pieces
1 small red onion, sliced thinly in rings and separated

DRESSING:
6 tablespoons extra virgin olive oil
3 tablespoons red wine vinegar
2 tablespoons Creole Mustard, commercial or
  see recipe page 74
2 teaspoons Dijon-style mustard, commercial or
  see recipe page 68
1 teaspoon dry mustard mixed with
  2 teaspoons cold water
1/4 teaspoon dried thyme
Salt and freshly ground black pepper

Put the shrimp in a large bowl, and toss with the Creole seasoning or Cajun spice mix to coat well. Marinate the shrimp for thirty minutes at room temperature.

Heat a heavy skillet over medium-high heat, add the oil, and when hot, add the shrimp and saute it for about three minutes or until just done, being careful not to overcook or it will toughen. Let the shrimp cool.

Combine the spinach with the onion in a large salad bowl. Top with the shrimp, and chill.

To make the dressing, whisk the olive oil, vinegar, three mustards, and thyme together in a saucepan. Season the dressing with salt and pepper. Bring the mixture to a boil over medium heat, stirring constantly, until all the ingredients are combined and the dressing is hot.

Pour the hot dressing over the salad, and toss to coat well. Garnish with the onion rings, and serve.

Yield: 4 servings   **Heat scale:** Medium

MUSTARD DILL BREAD

This recipe was provided by my good friend Jeff Gerlach, the author of *Men's Guide to Bread Machine Baking*. He describes the bread as, "begging for some ham and cheese." Easy to prepare, it can be made by hand or in a bread machine. If made in a machine, follow the manufacturer's directions. Note: This recipe requires advance preparation.

1½ teaspoons active dry yeast
1/2 cup plus 2 tablespoons very warm water,
    110 to 115 degrees
3 cups bread flour
2 tablespoons dry milk powder
1 tablespoon sugar
3/4 teaspoon salt
1 tablespoon Dijon-style mustard, commercial or
    see recipe page 68
1 tablespoon melted margarine
2 teaspoons dill weed, or substitute dill seeds

Put the warm water in a small bowl, sprinkle the yeast over the top, and let stand for five minutes or until the yeast dissolves.

Combine all the remaining ingredients and mix, using your hands if necessary. Add the yeast, and continue to mix until the dough comes together, adding more flour or water if needed.

Turn the dough onto a floured board, and knead until it is smooth and elastic.

Place the dough in an oiled mixing bowl, cover loosely with plastic wrap, and let rise in a warm place until doubled, about an hour to an hour and a half.

Oil a 1-pound loaf pan. Punch the dough down, and form it into a loaf. Place the dough in the pan, and let rise until doubled again.

Preheat the oven to 350 degrees. Bake the bread for thirty-five to forty minutes or until the top is browned and the bottom sounds hollow when tapped. Turn onto a rack to cool.

Yield: 1 pound loaf   **Heat scale:** Mild

All Kinds of Pepper

PIPER NIGRUM, COMMONLY CALLED BLACK PEPPER

The world of black pepper ranges from the mundane—a shaker of bland, finely ground pepper on a Formica tabletop at a truck stop—to the exotic: its bizarre history, complex chemistry, and vines of pungent berries climbing tall poles on faraway tropical islands. Interestingly, a popular history and cookbook devoted solely to black pepper has yet to be written, so until one is published, this treatise will have to suffice.

The word pepper originated with the Sanskrit (and later, Hindi) *pippali*, which at first referred to long pepper. It was transliterated as *péperi* in Greek, *piper* in Latin, and finally pepper in English, *pfeffer* in German, and *poivre* in French.

The long peppers of India and Indonesia come from slender climbers that have sparser-looking foliage than *P. nigrum*, the most noticeable difference between the two being that the fruits of Indian long pepper *(P. longum)* are smaller and less pungent than those of Javanese long pepper *(P. retrofractum)*. Long pepper is so called because the cylindrical spike fruits are 5 millimeters in diameter and 2.5 to 4 centimeters long.

THE PLANT AND ITS PUNGENCY

The *Piper* genus contains more than a thousand species of shrubs, vines, and small trees. It is part of the *Piperaceae* family which also includes the *Peperomia* genus of ornamental house plants. There are numerous cultivated varieties of *Piper nigrum*—more than seventy-five are grown in India alone, with the most popular being "Karimunda." The plant is a hardy, somewhat woody, perennial evergreen vine that grows in tropical climates. It can climb to 30 feet but is usually restricted to 10 to 15 feet under cultivation.

The oval, dark green leaves can reach 7 inches long by 4 inches wide. The flowers are borne at the node and form into spikes that have fifty to a hundred fifty yellowish florets which are usually hermaphroditic, but sometimes unisexual with staminate and pistillate flowers on the same plant or on different plants. Flowering begins at the base and spreads to the top of the vine in about a week. Pollination occurs mostly during rainfall. The fruit, variously called a corn or berry, is 1/5 to 1/4 inch in diameter and is harvested when green or orange just turning to red.

On commercial plantations, the plants flower in May and June, and the berries are ready for picking from November to March in the Northern Hemisphere. Ladders are placed against the posts, and workers carefully hand-pick the spikes at the optimum ripeness for whichever type of pepper is being processed. They place the spikes in mesh bags tied around their waists, and then either the spikes are processed into green pepper or the berries are stripped from the spikes and dried in the sun on woven mats or concrete slabs. During the drying process, the piperine in the berries turns the pericarp (outer skin) black and forms the volatile and nonvolatile oils. The sun dries out the berries, turning them wrinkled and black. Solar dryers and wood-burning furnaces are also used.

To make green peppercorns, the freshly picked spikes are stripped of their berries, and the berries are pickled in vinegar or brine. They are also freeze-dried, a process that results in green peppercorn that are closest in color and flavor to the freshly picked ones. This process also results in the most costly green peppercorns. In addition, green peppercorns are simply dehydrated. The green berries are boiled for twenty minutes to kill the piperine, then dehydrated in the sun, turning a pale green color. Interestingly, some pepper plantations treat ripened red berries in the same manner, creating red pepper (not to be confused with pink "peppercorns"). This is more pungent than green pepper but is a very rare commodity.

To make white pepper, slightly more mature berries are submerged in water for several days to soften the pericarp (outer skin), which is then rubbed off. After that, the inner core is dried in the sun. White pepper's whiteness will increase if the peppercorns are soaked in running water. It is also possible to produce a form of white pepper from dried black peppercorns by grinding off the black pericarp in a machine, forming "decorticated black pepper." The color is identical to that of white pepper, but the flavor is closer to that of black pepper.

After drying, both black and white peppercorns are graded based on their weight, size, volatile oil content, and area of origin. "Pinheads," or immature berries, are limited in grade, as are "light" berries, empty berries that float when placed in water.

Pepper contains the alkaloid piperine, which gives peppers their characteristic aroma, flavor, and pungency. About 5 percent is present in black pepper, and 6 percent in long pepper. It is perceived on the lips and the front of the tongue. Piperine is not nearly as pungent as capsaicin; a 100 parts per million solution is roughly equivalent to a one or two parts per million solution of capsaicin.

The major extractive is called oleoresin black pepper, and is important in food manufacturing. It is extracted from the pepper with solvents such as hexane, which are evaporated off so that a thick oil is left. The bouquet comes from the volatile essential oil, and the bite comes from nonvolatile piperine.

Black pepper oil is made when the peppercorns are crushed and undergo steam distillation. The oil is used in herbal medicine and aromatherapy. Amazingly, up to a half-ton of peppercorns must be processed to yield a single quart of black pepper oil, resulting in retail prices in 2002 of about $20 for one-third ounce.

PEPPER IN THE CLINIC AND THE KITCHEN

Generally speaking, pepper is consumed in such small quantities as a spice that it will not do much to fulfill the minimum daily requirements of nutrients needed by the human body. That said, black peppercorns are composed of about 50 percent carbohydrates and significant amounts of protein and fiber but only 3 percent fat. They also contain small quantities of calcium, iron, magnesium, phosphorous, potassium, sodium, niacin, vitamin C, and vitamin A.

FORMS

Green peppercorns are berries that are picked green, then dehydrated, freeze-dried, or liquid-packed. The place of origin is usually not indicated. They have a green, "herbal" flavor and a pungency that affects the nose, much like horseradish. The main sources are Madagascar, India, and Brazil.

Black pepper is the generic term for peppercorns that are picked green, just as they are starting to turn red. They are fermented briefly, then sun-dried so that the outer skin turns black while the inside remains pale.

White pepper is made from freshly picked green peppercorns that are soaked in water to remove the pericarp. The whitish peppercorns that are left are sun-dried. The white pepper of the port of Muntok on the island of Bangka off the southwest coast of Sumatra in Indonesia is considered to be finest.

PRINCIPAL TYPES IN COMMERCE

Black pepper is named for the area where it is grown or the port from which it is shipped.

- **Brazilian** peppercorns are noted for the smooth surface of the berries. They are one of the main sources of U.S. imports.
- **Lampong** is principally from the island of Sumatra in Indonesia. It has uniform berries and is highly pungent.

- **Malabar** is from the state of Kerala in India. All Indian pepper is generally called Malabar, which is quite pungent with a resinous aroma
- **Sarawak** is from Malaysia and is one of the principal peppercorns of commerce. It has small, light-colored peppercorns.
- **Tellicherry** is also from India, and is any Malabar pepper that has large berries. It is less pungent than other Malabars, which are considered to be the most complex in flavor.

Other principal black pepper-growing countries are Vietnam, Ceylon, Thailand, Nigeria, and China.

White pepper is named for the country where it is grown or the port from which it is shipped.

- **Muntok** is from Indonesia, where all the crop of the island of Bangka is used for white pepper production; this pepper is relatively mild.
- **Brazilian** pepper is lighter in color and less pungent than the Muntok variety. Most of it is exported to Argentina and Western Europe, with minor quantities to the U.S.
- **Sarawak** is exported exclusively to the British Commonwealth, Europe, and Southeast Asia. It is light in color and very mild in flavor.

COMMERCIAL PEPPER PREPARATIONS

Numerous manufacturers produce every conceivable blend of various peppercorns, often including pink "peppercorns." Additionally, there are pepper products combined with other ingredients, including:

- **Lemon Pepper Blend:** Ground black and white peppercorns and dehydrated ground lemon peel.
- **Garlic Pepper Blend:** Ground black and white peppercorns and dehydrated ground garlic.
- **Onion Pepper Blend:** Ground black and white peppercorns and dehydrated ground onion.
- **Sarawak Green Pepper Sauce:** A product of Malaysia, this contains green peppercorns ground to a purée and mixed with vinegar, salt, sugar, and spices.

SELECTING PEPPER

When buying pepper, consider what is the most important characteristic you are looking for. Is it pungency, bouquet, or appearance in the food being prepared? Here is a brief buying guide for the basic forms of pepper.

- **Green:** Available freeze-dried, dehydrated, and brined or vinegar-packed. Select containers with medium-size, whole berries. If in a liquid, make sure the liquid is clear.
- **Black:** Always buy unbroken, uniform, debris-free peppercorns. Go for the largest, freshest, full-scented peppercorns, although some, like Tellicherry, are so subtle that the aroma is not apparent until the peppercorns are cracked
- **White:** Look for whole, uncracked berries and uniform color.
- **Grinds:** Once ground, peppercorns quickly lose their flavor and pungency. They are designated by the size mesh the particles must pass through. For example, a 10-mesh screen has 10 openings per linear inch, and a 30-mesh screen has 30. The coarser the grind, the longer the pepper will last. Buy only uniformly ground pepper, and look for a sell-by date.

STORAGE

All pepper should be stored in an airtight, glass container (never plastic) out of direct light and away from any moisture source. Black peppercorns will last indefinitely when properly stored, but the shelf life of white pepper and coarsely ground black pepper is about a year. Green peppercorns packed in vinegar or brine will last about a month in the refrigerator, while water-packed ones should be used within a week.

GRINDING

All experts on the subject say to avoid buying ground pepper and always grind your own. The peppercorns then release their volatile oils and pungency.

To grind peppercorns of all kinds, you can use a mortar and pestle, but the method is labor intensive and will not grind evenly or finely. A ceramic mortar and pestle is preferred over a wooden one because wood absorbs the flavors of what is being ground and can produce off-flavors in subsequent grindings. Electric spice mills and coffee grinders can also be used, but there are very specific tools for grinding peppercorns.

During our research, we uncovered an enormous selection of peppermills and pepper grinders. The best ones have a ceramic grinding surface and a grind adjustment. Whether one is manual, electric, or electronic doesn't affect the fineness, taste, or pungency of the result. Antique peppermills are highly prized collectibles in Europe and are catching on in the U.S. The huge selection we found included:

- **Shapes:** cylinder, square tall wine bottle, tall restaurant, Turkish mill, triangle, hexagonal, globe, alien space pilot, beehive, Christmas ornament, chess pieces (all of them), botanic garden, bowling pin, teapot, lathe-turned, fine art sculpture, gourd, serpent;

- **Plastics:** Acrylics, Lexan;
- **Woods:** walnut, beechwood, maple, ebony, various laminated, teak, olive wood;
- **Metals:** brass, pewter, copper, stainless steel, gold, chrome, sterling silver, silver and crystal, aluminum;
- **Type:** manual, electric, electronic, with a light, pedestal, one-handed, obnoxious waiter with sound, mini-traveler, antique Victorian;
- **Countries:** Italy, Germany, Denmark, France, Greece, U.K., U.S.;
- **Colors:** black, purple, emerald, candy apple red, clear, green, blue, yellow, silver;
- **Grinding surface:** metal, zinc alloy, ceramic;
- **Age:** 1892–present;
- **Prices:** $19.95 to $200, $375 for an antique.

MIXING DIFFERENT TYPES OF PEPPER

Grind black, white, and pink peppercorns together with coriander seeds to add a dimension to smoked meats and fish and vegetables such as corn, winter squash, and sweet potatoes.

CULINARY USAGE

Pepper is one of the most universally used flavoring agents, appearing in processed meats, fish, vegetables, mayonnaise, fish crackers, vinegar, tea, coffee, liquor, Worcestershire sauce, salad dressings, and many other foods.

USE IN SAUCES

Green peppercorns are often combined with meat stock and liquor such as bourbon to make a sauce that is served over grilled lamb or veal chops. They are also used in salad dressings and soups.

Use in Baking

Most bakers prefer white pepper, which is more subtle when used in cakes, muffins, and focaccia. Other baked goods that benefit from using white (and in some cases, black) pepper include pastries, tart shells, vegetable breads such as pumpkin or zucchini, carrot cake, biscuits, and cookies.

Use in Desserts

One of the most common modern uses of cracked black pepper is in simple desserts. Long used in gingerbread, black pepper is being used by chefs today sprinkled over fruits such as berries, mango, pineapple, melon slices of all kinds, and orange sections.

Black Pepper Recipes

CRACKED BLACK PEPPER SUGAR ALMONDS

Caution: These sweet and spicy nuts are addictive! The more you eat, the spicier they get, and you need to eat more than one to get the full flavor. And the more you eat, the more you want to eat! They are a tasty, crunchy addition to accompany a buffet table or party.

        1 cup raw almonds
        2 teaspoons cracked black pepper
        1/2 teaspoon garlic salt
        1 tablespoon butter
        1/4 cup brown sugar

Preheat the oven to 350 degrees, line an 8-by-8-inch baking pan with aluminum foil, and lightly butter.

Combine the pepper and garlic salt in a bowl, and stir to mix.

Heat a nonstick skillet over medium heat, add the butter, and when melted, add the sugar and stir in 2 teaspoons water. Simmer the mixture until the sugar melts. Add the nuts, and continue to cook until the sugar bubbles, becomes thick and syrupy, and coats the nuts, about five minutes.

Sprinkle the pepper mixture over the top of the nuts, and quickly toss to coat. Pour the mixture into the pan.

Put the pan in the oven, and roast until the nuts are golden brown, about ten minutes.

Remove the foil with the nuts, and place on a wire rack to cool. When the nuts are cool, break them apart and serve.

Store the nuts in an airtight container.

Yield: 1 cup   **Heat scale:** Mild

STEAK AUX TROIS POIVRES

This intriguing dish violates at least two laws Americans have concerning steak: Never season it heavily, and never fry it in a pan. But since the taste of this steak is so remarkable, we'll forget the rules. Three varieties of pepper are recommended, but it works just fine using only coarsely crushed black peppercorns. Varying the hot sauce used can produce peppered steaks with intriguingly different flavors. Also, experiment by using brown, red, or rose peppercorns. This main dish is excellent when served with a fresh spinach salad and twice-baked potatoes.

> 4 sirloin or New York strip steaks, at least 1 inch thick
> 2 tablespoons black peppercorns, coarsely crushed
> 1 tablespoon white pepper powder
> 1 tablespoon green peppercorns, crushed
> 1 teaspoon salt
> 4 tablespoons butter
> 1/4 cup Worcestershire sauce
> 1 teaspoon hot pepper sauce
> 1/4 cup brandy

Wrap the peppercorns in a cloth, and crush them with a pestle. (Grinding them in a peppermill makes the pepper too fine.)

Coat both sides of the steaks with the crushed peppercorns and the white pepper. Press the pepper into the steak with a blunt instrument, and leave the steaks out uncovered at room temperature for at least one hour.

Sprinkle the salt in a large skillet, and heat until it begins to turn brown. Sear the steaks on each side quickly. Add the butter, and cook the steaks for one minute on each side. Add the Worcestershire sauce and the hot sauce, and cook another one to three minutes per side, depending on the thickness of the steaks and the doneness desired. Pour the brandy over the steaks, wait ten seconds, and then set it aflame. When the flame goes out, remove the steaks to a serving platter. Reduce the remaining liquid in the skillet, and serve it over the steaks. The steaks should be served rare.

Variation: For a heavier sauce, add 1/4 cup cream after removing the steaks from the skillet.

Yield: 4 servings   **Heat scale:** Medium

ASIAN BLACK PEPPER-BRAISED SHORT RIBS

These slightly sweet, peppery ribs combine many of the intense flavors of the Chinese cuisine.

Although the list of ingredients is long, don't let them scare you off—this is not a difficult recipe to prepare. The long, slow cooking produces very tender ribs with a very complex sauce. Because they are so strongly flavored, serve these ribs with plain rice and vegetables.

2 pounds beef short ribs, cut in 2- to 3-inch lengths, fat trimmed
2 tablespoons vegetable oil, peanut preferred
1 tablespoon thinly sliced garlic
1 tablespoon thinly sliced ginger
2 tablespoons coarsely ground black pepper
2 tablespoons coarsely ground Sichuan pepper (fagara, available by mail order; if unavailable, substitute equal portions of anise and allspice)
3 star anise buttons
1½ cups unsalted beef broth
1 cup dry red wine
3 tablespoons Chinese vegetarian black vinegar, or substitute rice vinegar.
2 tablespoons dry mustard
2 tablespoons oyster sauce (available at Asian markets)
1 tablespoon brown sugar
1 teaspoon black bean sauce (available at Asian markets)
1/2 teaspoon Chinese Five-Spice Powder
1/4 cup chopped green onions
Garnish of toasted sesame seeds

Heat a heavy saucepan over high heat, add the ribs, and cook until they are browned on all sides. Remove the ribs, and keep warm. Pour off the accumulated fat.

Add the garlic, ginger, peppercorns, and anise to the pan, and saute for a couple of minutes. Add the wine, vinegar, mustard, oyster sauce, sugar, black bean sauce, and Five-Spice Powder, and bring to a boil.

Reduce the heat, return the beef to the pan, cover, and simmer for an hour or until the meat is very tender and the sauce has thickened. Skim any fat that accumulates off the sauce. Stir in half the onions, and cook for a couple of minutes longer.

To serve, place the ribs on a serving platter, pour sauce over the top, and garnish with the remaining green onions and the sesame seeds.

Yield: 4 servings   **Heat scale:** Medium

Peppercorn Pulao with Toasted Cumin Seeds

Pulao means pilaf, and refers to a dish that always has you brown the rice before cooking. This is a simple dish to prepare and is a wonderful accompaniment to meat, poultry, and fish—not just curries. The vermicelli and nuts give a nice flavor, and the mellow heat from the pepper complements other spicy dishes. We recommend using basmati rice in this recipe. Basmati is Sanskrit for "queen of fragrance," and the rice has a nut-like aroma and flavor which further enhances the taste of the *pulao*.

  2 tablespoons vegetable oil
  1 medium onion, one half chopped and one half
     thinly sliced
  2 teaspoons coarsely crushed black peppercorns
  1 teaspoon coarsely crushed cumin seeds
  1/4 teaspoons ground turmeric
  1/2 cup vermicelli, broken into 1-inch pieces
  3/4 cup basmati rice
  2 cups chicken or vegetable broth
  1 teaspoon salt
  3/4 cup frozen peas
  1 tablespoon butter
  1/3 cup cashews

Heat a heavy skillet over medium-high heat, add 1 tablespoon of the oil, and when hot, add the chopped onion and saute until soft but not browned. Add the pepper, cumin, and turmeric, and saute, stirring continuously, until fragrant, about one minute. Remove and place the mixture in a bowl.

Add the vermicelli to the skillet, and saute until golden. Add the rice, and continue to saute until the vermicelli is lightly browned. Add to the spice mixture.

Pour the broth into a large saucepan, and bring to a boil. Add the rice mixture and salt, and stir to mix. When the broth returns to a boil, reduce the heat, cover, and simmer until the rice is done, about twenty to thirty minutes. Stir in the peas, and cover until they have cooked, about five minutes.

Heat a small skillet over medium heat, add the butter and remaining oil, and when hot, add the sliced onions; saute until they start to brown, about eight minutes. Add the nuts and cook, stirring constantly, until they are golden brown, four to five minutes. Remove, and drain on paper towels.

Mound the rice on a platter or in a bowl, garnish with the toasted onions and cashews, and serve.

Yield: 4 servings   **Heat scale:** Mild

TANGERINE AND CRACKED BLACK PEPPER SORBET

Here's a sweet and spicy sorbet that will surprise and delight guests. Putting fruit and black pepper together may seem like a strange flavor combination, but the pepper actually enhances the fresh flavor of the tangerine. If you don't have an ice cream freezer, make a granita instead—a frozen dish with an intentionally grainy texture similar to that of shaved ice. Just follow the recipe but pour the mixture into a shallow metal dish, and place it in the freezer. Stir every hour to cause ice crystals to form until it is similar to shaved ice.

> 1 cup sugar
> 1/2 teaspoon lemon juice
> 4 cups tangerine juice, about 15 tangerines
> 1 tablespoon finely grated tangerine peel
> 1½ teaspoons freshly coarse-ground black pepper
> Garnish of fresh mint sprigs

Combine the sugar, 1 cup water, and lemon juice in a saucepan, and bring to a boil over medium heat. Reduce the heat, and simmer over low heat until all the sugar is dissolved and the mixture is clear. Skim off any foam that forms. Cool the syrup in the refrigerator.

When the syrup is cold, combine it with the tangerine juice, peel, and black pepper. Freeze the sorbet in an ice cream freezer according to the manufacturer's instructions.

Serve the sorbet in chilled martini glasses with a sprig of mint.

Yield: 6 to 8 servings   **Heat scale:** Mild

FRESH MARGARITA STRAWBERRIES WITH TEQUILA AND CRACKED BLACK PEPPERCORNS

Another flavor combination that may seem unusual is strawberries and black pepper, but the pepper will enhance the fresh flavor of the berries. If you don't want to use alcohol, simply leave out the tequila; the flavor will be different but still tasty. This quick and easy dessert has a sweet-and-sour taste, and the peppercorns leave your mouth warm after the strawberries. Denice Skrepcinski shared this recipe, and since she is a food stylist, she knows how to turn a simple bowl of fruit into a very special dessert.

> 4 cups sliced fresh strawberries
> 1/3 cup orange juice, fresh preferred
> 1/4 cup tequila, optional
> 2 tablespoons lime juice, fresh preferred
> 1 to 1½ teaspoons balsamic vinegar
> 1½ teaspoons freshly ground coarse black pepper
> Garnish of lime slices and sugar

Combine the strawberries, orange juice, tequila, lime juice, and vinegar, and toss to coat. Add the pepper, and toss again.

For a dramatic presentation, rub the rims of margarita glasses with lime juice, and dip them into the sugar. Divide the strawberries among the glasses, sprinkle a little sugar over the berries, garnish with lime slices, and serve.

Yield: 4 servings **Heat scale:** Mild

PART 4

Powders: Spice Blends, Rubs, and Curries

MAKING CHILE POWDERS

When turning fresh pods into powders, use a food dehydrator to dry them out before grinding. If they are dry enough to snap in half rather than bend, they are ready for grinding. Although whole pods keep best because they oxidize less and retain more color and flavor, the most storage-efficient way to store them is to grind them into powders. All dried chiles can be ground into powder—and most are, including the habanero.

Remember, though, that because small particles oxidize faster than pods, the powders must be stored properly. Crushed chiles, or those coarsely ground with some of the seeds, are called quebrado. Coarse powders are referred to as caribe, while the finer powders are termed molido. The milder powders, such as New Mexican, can also be used as the base for sauces, but the hotter powders such as cayenne and piquin are used when heat is needed more than flavor.

The pods should be dried and the seeds removed for more-pure powder colors. A short-cut for drying pods that will be immediately turned into powder is to cut the fresh pods of any size in half, remove the seeds, chop them coarsely, and then microwave small amounts on low power until most of the moisture is gone. Place these microwaved pepper pieces in a food dryer or under the sun until they break when bent. They can also be dried in a 200-degree oven for six to eight hours.

Remember that drying fresh peppers in the oven for long periods of time tends to darken them, and they have a tendency to lighten under full sun. The next step is to grind the peppers into powders. The fresher the powders, the better they taste, so don't grind up too many pods. Use an electric spice mill, and be sure to wear a painter's mask to protect the nose and throat from the pungent powder. Many cooks experiment by changing the powders called for in recipes.

Adventurous cooks can experiment with creating powders of specific colors. For example, collect the different varieties of green, yellow, orange, red, and brown chiles, and separate them into their respective colors. The colors of the powders vary from a bright, electric red-orange (chiltepíns) to light green (dried jalapeños) to a dark brown that verges on black (ancho). The colored powders can then be combined with spices, as in our recipe for Chili Powder (page 113), or they can be stored for later use.

Another use for the powders is to turn them into green, yellow, orange, red, or brown chile pastes. Since some of the colors of the powders tend to be a bit dull, they can be brightened up by adding a few drops of the appropriate food coloring when making the pastes. In some kitchens, there are more powders available than whole pods because the powders are concentrated and take up less storage space. Keep the powders in small, airtight bottles in the freezer for extended shelf life.

BARBECUE RUBS

Meat that is to be grilled or smoked is often treated with spice mixtures and marinades of various types before, during, and after the cooking process. Now, of course, there is a great debate in the contentious world of barbecue not only about which of these marinades to use but also over whether to use them in the first place. Many grillers, for example, would never use a rub on their sirloin steak. And you'll hear time and time again from the smoking purists: Good barbecue doesn't need condiments. No rubs, no marinades, no sops, no sauces. If that's so, please tell us why nearly every recipe you can find for Texas barbecued brisket contains at least two of these three steps:

- Massage a rub into the meat, and let stand for half an hour before smoking;
- Apply a sop during the smoking process;
- Serve the sliced meat topped with a barbecue sauce.

In some recipes, the sliced meat is mixed with the barbecue

sauce and allowed to sit before serving. In others, the meat sits in the sop, and barbecue sauces are omitted. Some barbecuers prefer just to use a rub, claiming that brisket and ribs get a better crust when a sop is used. What we are talking about here is personal preference. Cooking is more of an art than an exact science, which is why at any given time, there are tens of thousands of cookbooks containing millions of recipes!

Rubs are essentially dry spice mixtures. A rub can be as simple as crushed black pepper or as elaborate as a jerk or curry rub. Their purpose is to add intense flavor to the meat without excessive moisture. A paste is a rub with a little moisture—usually water, beer, or oil—added to bind it. Generally speaking, rubs are used more with meat and poultry and pastes more with seafood. A notable exception is Jamaican jerk pork, which can be treated with either a jerk rub, a jerk paste, or in some cases (mostly outside Jamaica), a jerk sauce.

The most important thing to remember about making rubs is to use the freshest possible ingredients, not the ground oregano that's been in your cupboard since 1986. Older spices and herbs oxidize, or turn rancid, and either lose their flavor or gain a flavor you don't want on your meat. Buy spices such as mustard, black pepper, cumin, and coriander in whole form, and grind them yourself. The same goes for chile peppers—buy the pods, not the powder. Spices should preferably be fresh, but we've bought some incredible dried Mexican oregano in bulk. Dry fresh spices in the microwave, and then crush them in a mortar.

You can use a spice mill, a coffee grinder, or a mortar and pestle to make the rubs, just remember not to grind the mixture too finely. The object is to keep the herbs and spices from releasing too much of their essential oils, which is caused by friction and the heat of the grinder motor.

Rubs—and particularly pastes—do not store all that well. If you must store a rub, put it in a small jar with a tight seal, and place it in a cool, dry cupboard, or in the freezer. Oxygen and light are the enemies of a rub. Pastes can be stored for a few days but only in the refrigerator.

Dry rubs are massaged into the meat or poultry, lightly covered, and allowed to sit for as little as a half-hour or as long as a day. When using pastes on seafood, completely cover the shrimp, fish, or whatever in the paste, then wrap it tightly in plastic to more fully infuse it with flavor. The same technique works with pastes applied to meat or poultry.

Debates continue to rage about the use of rubs in the barbecue process. Some people say the rub seals the meat, keeping the juices in, but others warn that salt in the rub will draw the juices out, and they will evaporate. (Note that most rubs have a little salt in them.) At least one home physicist theorizes that the dryness of the rub attracts moisture from the air and actually adds it to the meat, but this is doubtful. Barbecue writer Richard Langer explains that, "A rub draws a portion of the juices from a cut of meat to the surface, there to mingle with the seasoning and form a crust encasing the rest of the meat's juices and flavors."

But food chemistry expert Harold McGee disagrees: "Any crust that forms around the surface of the meat is not waterproof." So it seems that if we use food common sense and don't add additional salt before smoking and don't worry about moisture loss because smoked meats are *supposed* to lose moisture as they tenderize, what happens is that the rubs simply add flavor and help make a tasty crust, or burnt end, or bark, as the barbecuers call the crust on the thin end of the brisket.

WORLDWIDE CURRY

Curries are by far the most wide-ranging spice mixtures in the world, so we've done quite a bit of research on the subject. People mistakenly think all curries are the same, but this is simply not true and reflects the similarity of dishes cooked with commercial curry powders. During the research for this book, we kept track of every single ingredient that appeared in curries throughout the world, from *ajowan* (bishop's weed) to yogurt. Then we eliminated the common meats, fruits, and vegetables, and still counted sixty-six separate ingredients, not including the different types of chile peppers and black pepper.

Such a huge number of ingredients means that curries are enormously varied. "Contrary to popular belief," notes Sri Lankan food importer Anura Saparamadu, "there are about as many types of curries as there are spices." And given the total number of curry ingredients, the combinations and permutations of those ingredients provide a nearly infinite variety of flavors in curries. "Even the best Indian cooks will argue endlessly over the inclusion and exclusion of particular spices and herbs," adds Santha Rama Rau, author of *The Cooking of India*.

During my travels, I have dined on curries in India, England, Thailand, Singapore, Malaysia, Australia, Jamaica, and Trinidad, in addition to those made at many Indian restaurants in the United States. We can testify by placing our right hands on this Bible that curries made with fresh ingredients are some of the tastiest culinary creations ever cooked up.

CURRY STYLES

Curry is a style of cooking and a spice mixture of nearly infinite variations. Other Indian spice mixtures include:

- Chat masala, a potato seasoning made with ground asafoetida, mint, ginger, ajowan, cayenne, salt, mango powder, cumin, and dried pomegranate seeds;
- Garam masala, a spice mixture from northern India similar to curry powder and used to flavor meats and vegetables; it contains cumin, coriander, cardamom, black peppercorns, cloves, mace, bay leaf, and cinnamon;

- Panch panora, a seed and spice mixture used on fried potatoes that contains brown mustard, nigella, cumin, fenugreek, and fennel seed;
- Sambhar powder, used in South Indian soups and containing coriander seed, besan flour, cumin seed, black peppercorns, salt, fenugreek, brown mustard seed, chile powder, cinnamon, turmeric, curry leaves, and asafoetida powder;
- Tea spice, which is used to flavor tea and contains ground ginger, black pepper, mint, cardamom, cloves, and nutmeg.

FORMS OF CURRY

Many purists abhor commercial curry powders. "They are anathema to Indian cooking," wrote Dharamjit Singh, author of *Indian Cookery*, "prepared for imaginary palates, having neither the delicacy nor the perfume of flowers and sweet-smelling herbs, nor the savour and taste of genuine aromatics." He added: "Curry powders often contain inferior spices which with age become acrid and medicinal in taste. They not only mask the natural taste of foods but lend a weary sameness to everything with which they are used."

Pat Chapman notes another drawback to commercial powders. "The manufacturers," he writes, "often put in too much chile and salt, and in some cases, chemical colorings and preservatives. Undeclared additives can include husks, stalks, and other adulterations." (In India, salt is added to curry powder to delay the formation of mold.)

Noted gastronome Elizabeth David also disliked prepared curry powders. "To me, they are unlikeable," she wrote, "harshly flavored and possessed of an aroma clinging and all-pervading in its way as English boiled cabbage or cauliflower. Too much hot red pepper, too much low-grade ginger, too much mustard seed and fenugreek. . . ."

Juel Anderson, author of *The Curry Primer*, has pointed out: "Through time, commercial spice mixtures have become so uniform a blend that most of us know curries only as yellow-colored foods with a standard aroma, often peppery-hot and as predictable in flavor as a Big Mac." Indeed, there is a sameness to commercial curry powders, especially those made in the United States to the 1977 U.S. Department of Agriculture standards for curry powder, which call for the following percentages of spices: coriander, 36; turmeric, 28; cumin, 10; fenugreek, 10; white pepper, 5; allspice, 4; mustard, 3; red pepper, 2; and ginger, 2.

However, we should point out that many imported curry powders, especially from India, vary considerably in flavor because they contain a wider variety of spices used in many different percentages.

Commercial curry powders are basically convenience condiments, and should be treated that way. John Philips Cranwell suggests three reasons for using commercial curry preparations: They produce a uniform result with a given recipe; the individual spices necessary to make a certain curry may not be available at a given time; and buying commercial curry preparations saves kitchen time and work.

We believe that common sense must prevail. It may be true, as Dharamjit Singh suggests, that: "Once you have tried [separate spices], you will no more use the packaged curry powder than you would accept another person's taste in the choice of your clothes." But, on the other hand, is it bad to use a packaged Sri Lankan curry paste if the cook has run out of some of the necessary ingredients to prepare a fresh curry paste? Or if fresh lemongrass is not immediately available for a Thai curry, should the cook substitute powdered lemongrass or use a packaged curry paste containing fresh lemongrass? These are decisions only the cook can make, and there will certainly be times when convenience will triumph over authenticity.

Our recommendation is that whenever possible, cooks should use freshly ground or mixed ingredients for their curries. Prepared powders and other products can be a backup for cooks who lack the time or certain essential ingredients, but cooks should, whenever possible, avoid the cheap American curry powders.

Generally speaking, the commercial curry preparations fall into the following categories. *Masalas* are spice blends that usually lack turmeric. *Curry powders* contain turmeric (the yellower the powder, the more turmeric it contains), and a large percentage of coriander. Imported powders are generally superior to domestic ones. *Curry pastes* are sealed, moist blends of herbs, spices, and other ingredients such as coconut, onions, fresh chiles, and ginger. They are imported from India, Thailand, Indonesia, and Sri Lanka. *Curry sauces* are available either in bottles or mixes, and are used as marinades or to make an "instant" curry gravy for meats. *Curry oils* are vegetable oils steeped in curry spices, and they are generally used as a condiment to add a curry flavor to prepared foods.

MAKING FRESHLY GROUND CURRY POWDERS

Since the process of making a powder exposes more surface area of a spice as it is ground, the spice oxidizes more quickly in powder form, quickly losing volatile oils and flavor components. We advise cooks to make only enough powder to cook one meal and to avoid storing leftover powder. However, we realize that some cooks will make quite a volume of powder and, being frugal, will store it. In this case, we advise using as small a jar as possible and sealing the top tightly.

Curry pastes store better than powders because the moisture in them retards oxidation and traps the spice oils. But the moisture is also a breeding ground for fungi and bacteria, so curry pastes should always be refrigerated. Some cooks place a thin layer of vegetable oil over the paste to reduce oxidation even more.

The first step in making curry powder is to roast the raw spices. This is accomplished by placing them in a dry skillet on top of the stove, in a dry electric frying pan, or on a baking sheet placed under the broiler or in the oven. The goal is to heat the spices with medium heat until they release their distinct aromas. Except in the cases of some dark curry blends, such as those from Sri Lanka, the spices should not be blackened. Also, they should not be heated for too long, or the volatile oils will be lost. Practice is the only way to learn how long to roast the spices. The oily and volatile spices, such as cloves, cinnamon, cardamom, and mace, are usually not roasted—but there are exceptions in some recipes.

The next step is grinding the spices. Cooks have several options, including the original method of grinding between two stones, which in this day and age is a bit obsolete. A mortar and pestle can be used, but it takes a lot of muscle power to grind the spices fine enough to make a powder. Blenders, coffee grinders, and food processors may also be used, but by far, the best solution is to use an electric mill dedicated only to spices. Grind the roasted spices in small quantities so as not to burn out the motor. Avoid grinding whole dried ginger or turmeric without first pulverizing it with a hammer, because it is very fibrous and difficult to grind with home equipment. Some cooks find it easier just to use powdered ginger and turmeric.

Freshly ground spices can be stored for later use but not for long periods of time. Two or three months is the maximum for most ground spices; be sure to store them in small bottles, tightly capped, in a dark place, as sunlight can degrade the flavors.

Blending the roasted and ground spices is simple. Either use the spice mill, or place the spices in a shallow bowl and blend them thoroughly with a fork.

Use a food processor or blender to make curry pastes, following the individual recipe directions. Often, pastes must be made in two or three batches, and then further mixed by hand. Some pastes must be fried in oil before they are added to the recipe. This procedure removes water from the onions and other paste ingredients and cooks the spices again to remove their raw flavor. Just take care not to burn the paste.

COOKING AND SERVING CURRIES

Some cooks suggest that curry spices actually take a secondary role to the other ingredients. "Although the dish is called curry," observes Julie Sahni, "the most characteristic ingredient in all classic curries is the slowly cooked, caramelized onions not unlike those used in French onion soup." Indeed, in many cuisines, the curry spices used provide only a portion of the flavor of the dish. Additional tastes are contributed by lemongrass, galangal, coconut, papaya, tamarind, or other exotic ingredients. And finally, the chosen meats, fish, or vegetables in the curry also add their unique flavors.

Most curries are cooked in large skillets or woks, so the curry cook is advised to have a selection of shallow, non-aluminum cookware with lids. Wooden spoons are the best utensils for stirring curries, since they do not conduct heat very well.

Curries are convenient to cook for parties since most can easily be prepared ahead of time and reheated just before serving. They also freeze well, which is a great convenience. Cooks should remember that some curries, such as salads, can be served cold and make good outdoor summer food.

And what other dishes should be served with curries? Most curries are served with some form of rice, and plain white rice is an excellent accompaniment. Basic condiments often served with curries worldwide are fried eggplant, tamarind jam, candied coconut, candied ginger, pickled vegetables (such as onions), mango chutney, grated fresh coconut, grated roasted coconut, chopped peanuts or almonds, grated or sliced hard-boiled eggs, chopped crisp bacon, chopped tomatoes, and salted fish. The condiments are usually either served in bowls, so that guests may sprinkle them over the curry, or are placed on the side of the individual dishes.

Spice Mix Recipes

ANCHO CHILE DRY RUB

Here's a great rub to use on meats that will be smoked or grilled. Since anchos are sold in fairly pliable condition, place them in the oven on low heat until they are brittle.

4 ancho chiles, stems removed and seeded,
   dried in the oven
2 teaspoons whole white peppercorns
1 teaspoon whole black peppercorns
1/2 teaspoon celery seed
3½ teaspoons cumin seed
1 teaspoon thyme
1 small bay leaf
1 teaspoon annato seeds
1½ teaspoons salt

Combine all the ingredients in a spice mill or blender. Pack in a glass jar after using.

Yield: About 1/2 cup   **Heat scale:** Mild

Chili Powder

This powder is used to make chili con carne, and replaces the commercial type; experiment with the ingredients, and adjust them to your taste.

    5 tablespoons ground New Mexican red chile
    1 tablespoon ground hot chile, such as
        piquin or chiltepín
    1½ tablespoons ground cumin
    1½ tablespoons ground oregano
    1½ tablespoons garlic powder
    1 teaspoon salt

Mix all the ingredients together, and process in a blender or spice grinder until fine. Store the excess powder in a glass jar.

Yield: 1/2 cup   **Heat scale:** Hot

DRY JERK SEASONING

Jerk seasoning is actually a delicious, tropical way to barbecue. Use it to season either pork or poultry; simply rub it into the meat, marinate overnight in the refrigerator, grill (or bake), and then enjoy!

1 teaspoon dried ground habanero chile, or
    substitute other hot powder such as cayenne
2 tablespoons onion powder
2 teaspoons ground thyme
2 teaspoons ground allspice
1 teaspoon coarsely ground black pepper
1/2 teaspoon ground nutmeg
1/2 teaspoon ground cinnamon
1/2 teaspoon garlic powder
1/4 teaspoon ground cloves

Combine all the ingredients and mix well. Store the extra seasoning in a glass jar.

Yield: About 1/4 cup   **Heat scale:** Hot

BAFAT
(HURRY CURRY)

There are scores of curry powders on the market today. Though purists may frown on them, they are indeed useful for making curries in a hurry. Even in India, curry powders have become an integral part of middle-class family life. The following curry powder, called *bafat,* is from southwestern India, and can be used for a meat, fish, or vegetable dish. It can even be used the same day for two completely different dishes, each with its own unique flavor!

1/3 cup coriander seeds
1/4 cup cumin seeds
2 tablespoons mustard seeds
2 tablespoons peppercorns
2 tablespoons whole cloves
1 tablespoon fenugreek seeds
2 tablespoons ground cardamom
2 tablespoons ground cinnamon
2 tablespoons powdered turmeric
1/4 cup freshly ground, hot red chile powder

Dry the whole spices on a cookie sheet in the oven at 200 degrees for fifteen minutes, taking care they do not burn. Remove them from the oven, cool, and grind them in a spice mill in small batches. Combine them with the ground spices in a bowl, and mix well. Store the curry powder in an airtight container.

Yield: About 1 1/2 cups   **Heat scale:** Hot

NAM PRIK GAENG PED
THAI RED CURRY PASTE

This spicy hot, flavorful paste from Thailand can be added to just about any curry, no matter what the country of origin, to give the dish another dimension. All the pastes are hot, and are used as a base in all the curries. This one gets its name from the Thai red chiles used, which can be either fresh or dried. If you are using dried, be sure to soak them in hot water to soften before processing. Traditionally, a mortar and pestle is used, but we've found it much easier to prepare using a modern blender or food processor. Galangal is a root similar to ginger but not quite as sweet, with a little hint of lemon, but since it can be difficult to find, ginger is an acceptable substitute. If you decrease the number of chiles to reduce the heat level, you may have to add paprika to maintain the characteristic red color.

1 tablespoon coriander seeds
1 teaspoon cumin seeds
1 teaspoon caraway seeds
1 teaspoon black peppercorns
10 to 15 red Thai chiles, stems and seeds removed, or
     substitute 10 small dried red chiles such as
     piquins, or japones
2 stalks fresh lemongrass
1 tablespoon chopped garlic
4 small shallots, thinly sliced
1 tablespoon coarsely grated galangal or ginger
Grated zest of 1 small lime
1/4 cup chopped fresh cilantro, including the stems
1 teaspoon shrimp paste (available in Asian markets)
1 teaspoon salt
2 to 4 tablespoons vegetable oil, peanut preferred, or
     more to form a paste

Heat a heavy skillet over high heat, add the coriander, cumin, caraway, and peppercorns, and dry roast until the seeds darken and become fragrant, being careful that they don't burn. Let the ingredients cool completely, and then place them in a spice mill or coffee grinder, and process to a fine powder.

Trim the stalks of the lemongrass to about 3 inches in length. Cut away any hard portions, discard the outer leaves, and coarsely chop.

Place all the ingredients except the oil in a blender or food processor, and with the motor running, slowly add just enough of the oil to form a paste.

Refrigerate for up to a month, or freeze for four months.

Yield: 1/2 cup   **Heat scale:** Hot

GOAN PORK VINDALOO

Vindaloo is a classic pork curry dish from the state of Goa, an area of India that was populated by Portuguese sailors who carried it on their long sea voyages. A layer of fat was placed on top to seal out air and help preserve the meat on these journeys. The word vindaloo is a combination of "vin," which means vinegar, and the Portuguese word for garlic, "albo," since the dish combines both of these in large amounts. According to Hindu philosophy, the spice combinations in the vindaloo are believed to purify, heal, and cool. Traditionally, vindaloos are very pungent and hot, actually the hottest of all the Indian curries, and since most Goans are Christians or Hindus, there is no taboo about eating pork.

4 dried red New Mexican chiles, stems and
   seeds removed
4 dried chile piquins, stems and seeds removed, or
   cayenne chiles
1 piece cinnamon stick, 2-inches, crushed
2 tablespoons coriander seeds
2 teaspoons cumin seeds
1 teaspoon fenugreek seeds
1 teaspoon black mustard seeds
1 teaspoon fennel seeds
10 black peppercorns
6 whole cloves
6 cloves garlic
2 tablespoons grated ginger
2 tablespoons vegetable oil
2 pounds boneless pork, trimmed and cut in 1-inch cubes
1/2 cup coconut vinegar (available in Indian markets)
   or distilled white vinegar
3 cups chopped onion
Garnish of grated coconut

Put the chiles in a bowl, cover them with very hot water, and allow them to steep fifteen minutes to soften. Drain the chiles, and discard the water.

Heat a heavy skillet over high heat, add the cinnamon, coriander, cumin, fenugreek, mustard, fennel, peppercorns, and cloves, and dry roast until the spices darken and become fragrant, being careful that they don't burn. Let the spices cool completely, and then place them in a spice mill or coffee grinder and process to a fine powder.

Place the chiles, spices, garlic, and ginger in a blender or food processor, and purée to a smooth paste, thinning with some of the vinegar if necessary.

Combine the pork, a little of the spice paste, and vinegar in a bowl, and toss to coat. Let the meat marinate at room temperature for thirty minutes.

Heat a heavy saucepan over medium-high heat, add the oil, and when hot, add the onions and saute until they are browned. Add the spice paste and saute for a couple of minutes, using a little water if the paste becomes too thick.

Add the meat to the saucepan and brown, being careful that the spices don't burn. Add 2 to 3 cups of water, bring to just below boiling, reduce the heat, cover, and simmer until the meat is fork tender, about one hour. Remove the lid, and turn up the heat to cook off any excess liquid.

To serve, mound cooked rice on a serving platter, top with the vindaloo, and garnish with the coconut.

Yield: 4 servings   **Heat scale:** Medium to hot

JAMAICAN JERK PORK

The "jerk" in jerk pork is a spice mixture that was used to preserve meat before refrigeration. It was developed by the Awarak Indians, and later refined in Jamaica by runaway slaves known as Maroons. These days, the spices are used to season meats for barbecue and to tenderize rather than preserve. An inexpensive smoker or a covered grill can be substituted for the traditional jerk pit, and is a lot easier than digging a hole in your backyard. Just sit back and enjoy a rum punch or cold beer while tending your pork! Note: This recipe requires advance preparation

1 pork butt, 3- to 4-pounds, or loin roast

JERK PASTE:

3 to 4 Scotch bonnet chiles, stems and seeds removed,
    chopped, or substitute habanero chiles

1/4 cup chopped green onions, including some of
    the greens

1/4 cup crushed allspice (pimento) berries, or substitute
    2 teaspoons ground

3 tablespoons fresh thyme

3 cloves garlic

2 tablespoons grated ginger

2 tablespoons lime juice, fresh preferred

2 tablespoons red wine vinegar

2 bay leaves

3 teaspoons freshly ground black pepper

2 teaspoons ground cardamom

1 teaspoon ground cinnamon

1 teaspoon ground nutmeg

1 teaspoon salt

3 to 4 tablespoons vegetable oil

To make the jerk paste, either pound the ingredients together with a mortar and pestle or use a blender or food processor. With the motor running, slowly add enough of the oil to make a paste.

Place the roast, fat side down, in a nonreactive pan. Make slashes in the pork about 1 1/2 to 2 inches apart and almost through the roast. Rub the jerk over the meat, making sure to get it thoroughly into the slashes. Cover with plastic wrap, and marinate in the refrigerator overnight.

Remove the roast, and bring to room temperature.

Prepare either the grill or smoker. If using a grill, be sure to use a pan under the pork to catch the drippings so they don't flare up and burn the meat. Smoke the pork for about two to three hours, turning the roast every thirty minutes to ensure even browning. Cook until a meat thermometer inserted into the thickest part registers 150 degrees. Let the meat sit for ten minutes to reabsorb all the juices and for the temperature to rise to 160 degrees.

Carve the meat, although it should be so tender it falls apart, mound it on a serving platter, and serve accompanied by cornbread, a tropical fruit salad, and a cold Red Stripe beer.

Variations: Substitute lamb chops, chicken, or turkey for the pork.

Yield: 4 servings   **Heat scale:** Hot

Texas "Chili Queen" Chili

There must be as many recipes for "chili" as there are cooks in Texas, New Mexico, and Arizona! Cooks seem to guard their recipes as if they were classified information. And every one of those states will declare that its is the best. Most chili aficionados will agree however, that the "chili queens" of San Antonio, Texas, were responsible for making the dish popular. In the 1880s, these women cooked up chili in big clay pots during the day and sold their wares from rickety chili stands on street corners all night long. From there, its fame spread, and soon, chili con carne began appearing on menus in Mexican restaurants all over Texas and elsewhere. In 1893, chili made its worldwide debut at the Chicago World's Fair, and the rest, as they say, is history. This recipe is our version of the classic San Antonio chili. Health-conscious cooks should prepare it the day before, chill it, and skim off any fat that rises. But even if you aren't concerned about the fat, the chili will taste better the next day.

6 dried red New Mexican chiles, stems and seeds removed

3 ancho chiles, stems and seeds removed

2 pounds coarse beef or sirloin, cut into 1-inch cubes

1 pound coarse pork or pork shoulder, cut into
    1-inch cubes

1 large onion, chopped

3 cloves garlic, minced

6 chiltepín chiles or piquins

1 tablespoon dried oregano, Mexican preferred

2 teaspoons cumin seeds

1 teaspoon sugar

1 quart beef broth

1 cup tomato sauce

Salt and freshly ground black pepper

2 cups cooked pinto beans, optional

Place the New Mexican and ancho chiles in a bowl, and cover them with very hot water. Let them steep for fifteen minutes to soften. Drain the chiles, and discard the water. Place the chiles in a blender or food processor along with some water, and purée them until smooth. Strain the mixture to remove any remaining pieces of chile skins.

Heat a heavy skillet over medium-high heat, add the meat, and saute until it browns. Drain off any excess fat that accumulates. Add a little vegetable oil to the skillet, and then brown the meat. Add the onions and garlic to the skillet, and continue cooking until the onions are soft, about ten minutes. Transfer the mixture to a large saucepan or stock pot.

Heat the pan over medium heat, crumble the chiltepíns over the mixture, and add the oregano, cumin, sugar, broth, and tomato sauce. Simmer the chili for forty-five minutes.

Stir in the chile purée, season with salt and pepper, and continue to simmer for an additional thirty minutes. Taste and adjust the seasonings, and add cayenne chile to increase the heat if desired.

To serve, ladle the chili into bowls, and serve the beans on the side. Guests can add the beans to their chili if desired.

Yield: 6 to 8 servings   **Heat scale:** Medium hot

BARBECUED BRISKET

Red Caldwell, who wrote for *Chile Pepper* magazine in the early days when I was editor, developed this recipe. He notes: "Most barbecue in Texas revolves around beef, and more specifically, brisket. When you select your brisket, choose only 'packer-trimmed' briskets in the ten- to twelve-pound category. The smaller briskets don't have enough fat to tenderize them, and the larger ones *could* have come off of a tough old range bull that no amount of cooking will *ever* tenderize. Avoid closely trimmed or 'value packed' brisket pieces. The fat that was cut off to make 'em pretty is the very stuff that would have made 'em tender! All briskets have a fat cover on one side. Ignore this! Squeeze the thick end with both thumbs. When you've found the brisket with the smallest fat kernel, that's the one for you. Take it home and build your fire. While your fire is getting going—I build mine out of a mixture of mesquite and oak—rub your brisket with a dry 'rub.' Make sure that the meat is thoroughly coated. This helps seal the meat and adds a flavorful crust. Never use salt, as it dries and toughens the meat. Use tongs instead of a fork to turn the meat because piercing allows the juices to flow out, leaving a tougher brisket." I will observe that this recipe is not designed for BBQ cookoff competitions because it is overly sauced—which improves this cut of meat, in my opinion.

THE BRISKET:
1 brisket as described above

Lemon juice, about   to   cup per brisket

DRY RUB:
1 11-ounce can of fine ground, light chili powder

1 tablespoon ground Cayenne powder

2 tablespoons (rounded) black pepper

4 tablespoons (rounded) garlic powder

RED'S BASTING SAUCE:

1 pound butter or margarine

2 onions, peeled and thick-sliced

5 cloves garlic, peeled and crushed

1 12-ounce bottle of beer (Shiner Bock preferred)

1 bunch parsley tops, chopped

4 lemons, quartered

1 pint cooking oil

2 tablespoons commercial chili powder

1/2 teaspoon cayenne powder

1/4 cup Worcestershire sauce

2 bay leaves

Thoroughly coat all surfaces of the brisket with lemon juice, and rub in well. Combine all the dry ingredients in a bowl, and sprinkle generously all over the brisket, rubbing in well and making sure the brisket is entirely covered. Store leftover rub in the refrigerator in a tightly sealed container.

When the wood has burned down, move the coals to one side of the smoker, place the meat *away* from the direct heat, *fat side up* (letting gravity and nature do the basting), then close it. Some people add a pan of water near the coals to provide added moisture, but I don't. Now, *don't* touch the meat for about twelve hours. Just drink a few beers, cook a pot of beans, and tend your fire. You'd like to hold the temperature to around 210 degrees in the brisket-cooking area. Since "helpers" usually show up at the first whiff of smoke, you probably ought to put some of your leftover rub on a couple of racks of pork ribs, and toss them on the smoker, at the hotter end, and baste and turn them for four or five hours, just to keep the animals at bay.

To make the Basting Sauce, melt the butter in a pan, add the onions and garlic, and saute for four to five minutes to soften. Add the beer, squeeze in the lemon juice, and add the lemon rinds to the pot. When the foam subsides, add all the remaining ingredients, and bring to a boil. Reduce the heat to medium low, and simmer for twenty minutes. By the way, you'll notice that there are no tomatoes, ketchup, or sugar in this recipe. All of these things caramelize and burn quickly, giving the meat a *nasty* taste.

After the twelve hours are up, generously slather the brisket with the Basting Sauce (not a barbecue sauce), wrap it tightly in aluminum foil, and return it to the smoker. Close off all the air supply to the fire, and let the meat "set" there for three or four hours. This step really tenderizes the meat.

Remove the brisket from the foil, and slice it thinly against the grain. Serve your brisket with beans, coleslaw, jalapeños, onions, pickles, and plenty of bread. Cold beer or iced tea are the traditional beverages of choice.

Yield: About 8 to 16 servings for a ten-pound brisket, depending on the individual brisket and the size of the guests' appetites.
Heat scale: Mild

PART 5

Resources

FURTHER READING

• DeWitt, Dave and Paul W. Bosland. *The Complete Chile Pepper Book: Choosing, Growing, Preserving, and Cooking.* Portland, OR: Timber Press, 2009.

• DeWitt, Dave. *1001 Best Hot & Spicy Recipes.* Chicago: Surrey Books, 2010.

• DeWitt, Dave. *The Southwest Table: Traditional Foods from Texas, New Mexico, and Arizona.* New York: Lyons Press, 2011.

• DeWitt, Dave. *Dave DeWitt's Chile Trivia.* Albuquerque: Sunbelt Media, 2012.

SEED AND PLANT SOURCES

For seeds, go to the Chile Pepper Institute, **www.chilepepper institute.org**, Paul W. Bosland, publisher; Danise Coon, editor.

For 500 varieties of chile pepper bedding plants in season and fresh chile pods in the late summer and early fall, go to Cross Country Nurseries, **www.chileplants.com**, Janie Lamson, publisher.

WEBSITES

For detailed information on chile peppers around the world:

• The Fiery Foods and Barbecue SuperSite, **www.fiery-foods.com**, Dave DeWitt, publisher; Lois Manno, editor. This site has more than four hundred articles on chile varieties, gardening, history, cooking, and Q&As.

• The Chile Pepper Institute, **www.chilepepperinstitute.org**, Paul W. Bosland, publisher and director; Danise Coon, editor and assistant director. The shop at this site contains books, chile information, and the seeds for dozens of chile varieties.

• Pepperworld.com, **www.pepperworld.com** (German language), Harald Zoschke, publisher and editor. The site's many articles include European chile-growing information.

- The Chileman, **www.thechileman.org**, Mark McMillan, publisher and editor. This U.K. site contains the best glossary of chile pepper varieties, with about four thousand listed.
- Fatalii.net, **www.fatalii.net**, a Finnish site, in English, with extensive information about chile growing and bonsai chiles. Jukka Kilpinnen is the publisher and editor.
- The Burn! Blog, **www.burn-blog.com**, which keeps chileheads and BBQ freaks in touch with the latest news, personalities, and weirdness in the worlds of chile peppers, spiced-up foods, and barbecues

CHILE PEPPER SUPPLIERS AND ONLINE HOTSHOPS

MexGrocer, **www.MexGrocer.com**, has many varieties of worldwide chiles as dried pods and powders.

Melissa's/World Variety Produce, Inc., **www.melissas.com**, has worldwide fresh chiles in season, as well as a fine collection of dried pods and powders.

Peppers, **www.peppers.com**, has the best selection of chile pepper and barbecue products such as hot sauces, salsas, jams, cookies, candies, rubs, chili mixes—the list is very long.

ABOUT THE AUTHOR

If Dave DeWitt's life were a menu, it would feature dishes as diverse as alligator stew and apple pie à la mode—not to mention the beloved chile peppers that have become the basic ingredient of so many of his projects and accomplishments.

Since starting out in the electronic media, Dave has built careers as a businessman, educator, administrator, producer, on-camera personality, author, and publisher. Currently, in addition to serving as CEO of Sunbelt Shows and co-producer of the National Fiery Foods & Barbecue Show, Dave is always busy sharing his chile pepper expertise in as wide a range of forums as possible.

Besides writing more than forty books (mostly on fiery foods but also including novels, food histories, and travel guides), Dave is publisher of the Fiery Foods & BBQ Super Site (at **www.fieryfoods.com**), and was a founder of Chile Pepper magazine and Fiery Foods & Barbecue magazine.

From his beginning as a radio announcer, Dave went on to own audio/video production companies for which he wrote, produced, and voiced hundreds of radio and television commercials. After moving to New Mexico in 1974, he wrote and hosted the "Captain Space" TV show which beat out both "Saturday Night Live" and "Star Trek" in its Saturday midnight time slot, and, in an entirely different sphere, curated the Albuquerque Museum's 1984 exhibit *Edward S. Curtis in New Mexico*.

The interest in chile peppers and spicy foods that has helped make Dave one of the foremost authorities in the world has led to such best-sellers as *The Whole Chile Pepper Book, The Pepper Garden, The Hot Sauce Bible, The Chile Pepper Encyclopedia*, and *The Spicy Food Lover's Bible*. His latest book on the subject is *Chile Trivia*. As the ultimate testament to his fame and achievement, *The New York Times* has declared him to be "the Pope of Peppers."

Dave is an associate professor in Consumer and Environmental Sciences on the adjunct faculty of New Mexico State University, and also serves as chair of the Board of Regents of the New Mexico Farm and Ranch Heritage Museum.